WONDERFUL WORLD OF KNOWLEDGE

YEAR BOOK 1978

Disney's

Wonderful
World of
Knowledge

YEAR BOOK 1978

THE DANBURY PRESS

THE DANBURY PRESS

a division of Grolier Enterprises, Inc.

ROBERT B. CLARKE   *Publisher*

ISBN 0-7172-8121-3
The Library of Congress Catalog Card Number: 77-95545

Text on pages 14-17, 50-53, 84-87, 120-123,
and all Disney character illustrations
Copyright © 1978, Walt Disney Productions

CONTENTS

1977 AT A GLANCE

JANUARY 20. James Earl Carter, Jr., was sworn in as the 39th president of the United States. Walter F. Mondale was sworn in as the 42nd vice-president.

JANUARY 21. On his first full day in office, President Carter pardoned about 11,000 men who had refused to enter the armed forces during the Vietnam War.

FEBRUARY 6. Queen Elizabeth II of England observed her "Silver Jubilee"—the 25th anniversary of her accession to the throne.

MARCH 9. President Carter announced the end of the 17-year ban on American travel to Cuba, as well as the end of the bans on travel to Vietnam, Cambodia, and North Korea.

MARCH 20. Prime Minister Indira Gandhi and the Congress Party she headed were defeated in parliamentary elections. The Congress Party had controlled the Indian Government since India became an independent nation in 1947. (On March 24, Morarji R. Desai, 81-year-old head of the Janata Party, was sworn in as India's fourth prime minister.)

MARCH 30. The National Aeronautics and Space Administration (NASA) announced the discovery of at least five rings around the planet Uranus. The rings resemble those around the planet Saturn.

APRIL 20. President Carter presented a national energy plan to Congress. He called the energy crisis America's most serious problem.

MAY 17. In parliamentary elections in Israel, the Likud Party defeated the Labor Party, which had dominated the government since the founding of Israel in 1948. (On June 22, Menahem Begin, leader of the Likud, became prime minister.)

JUNE 15. In the first free parliamentary elections since 1936, the Spanish people voted for members of the Cortes (the Spanish parliament).

JUNE 19. John Nepomucene Neumann, a Bishop of Philadelphia, was declared a saint by Pope Paul VI. Bishop Neumann, who died in 1860, thus became the first male saint of the United States.

JUNE 27. The Republic of Djibouti became Africa's 49th independent country. The tiny nation, formerly known as the French Territory of the Afars and the Issas, had been under French rule for 115 years.

JULY 5. In Pakistan, the Army seized power and overthrew the government of Prime Minister Zulfikar Ali Bhutto.

JULY 13.   New York City suffered a great power failure and blackout. It lasted as long as 25 hours in some areas. Looters and arsonists caused millions of dollars worth of damage.

JULY 21.   In Sri Lanka, Prime Minister Sirimavo Bandaranaike and her governing Freedom Party were defeated in parliamentary elections. Bandaranaike, one of the few women in the world to hold such high office, had been prime minister for a total of 12 years, since 1960.

AUGUST 4.   A Department of Energy was added to the U.S. Cabinet. James R. Schlesinger was named secretary of the new department.

AUGUST 16.   The *Enterprise,* the first re-usable space shuttle, passed a major test. Manned by two pilots, the shuttle was carried piggyback on a jumbo jet to an altitude of 24,000 feet (7,300 meters). The *Enterprise* was then separated from the jet, and the pilots glide-landed it on a dry-lake runway in the Mojave Desert. The shuttle is designed to be rocketed into orbit around the earth, and then to return to earth and land like an airplane. It is expected that, in the 1980s, shuttles will ferry men and equipment to orbiting space stations and satellites. ☐ The *Arktica,* a Soviet nuclear-powered icebreaker, became the first surface ship to smash through the huge sheets of ice to reach the North Pole.

AUGUST 20.   The first of the U.S. Voyager spacecraft was launched on a course that will take it to the outer reaches of the solar system. If all goes

well, it will travel past Jupiter and Saturn, and perhaps Uranus in 1986. (A second Voyager was launched on September 5, 1977.)

SEPTEMBER 7. President Carter and Omar Torrijos Herrera, Panama's head of government, signed new Panama Canal treaties. If the treaties are approved by the U.S. Senate, full ownership of the Canal will pass to Panama on December 31, 1999.

NOVEMBER 1. President Carter signed into law a bill that will increase the minimum wage in stages from its present $2.30 an hour to $3.25 an hour in 1981. □ The United States withdrew from the International Labor Organization (I.L.O.), the oldest specialized agency of the United Nations, on the grounds that it had become too political.

NOVEMBER 8. It was announced that astronomers had discovered an object between Saturn and Uranus that is orbiting the sun. It could be part of an undiscovered belt of asteroids, or it could be the solar system's tenth and smallest planet. Because the object is so small—about one-tenth the size of Mercury—it is temporarily being described as a "mini-planet."

NOVEMBER 19-21. President Anwar el-Sadat of Egypt made a three-day trip to Israel. It was the first time that an Arab leader had visited Israel. In a joint interview at the end of the historic visit, Israeli Prime Minister Begin and Sadat pledged that there would be "no more war."

DECEMBER 26. Prime Minister Menahem Begin of Israel and Egyptian President Anwar el-Sadat ended a two-day conference in Ismailia, Egypt. It was the first time that an Israeli head of state had ever visited officially an Arab country.

Fine Feathered Phantom

It was a perfectly lovely spring afternoon, and Gus and Jaq were relaxing in a sunny corner of the castle. Jaq had a glass of lemonade at his elbow, and Gus was enjoying some of Suzy Mouse's molasses cookies.

All the castle windows had been thrown open to the fine weather, and Jaq winced as he heard sounds of quarreling from Drucilla's third-floor bedroom.

"Those two!" he said to Gus in disgust. "Here Cinderelly brings them along with her to live like queens, and they're still not happy. Yesterday Drucilly said Anastasie took her favorite necklace. I wonder what it's about today."

Up in Drucilla's room the quarrel was getting louder. "You pilfering pest! I didn't take your tawdry necklace, but you *did* take my ruby earring," accused Anastasia.

Drucilla was, for once, at a loss for words.

"Can't think of a good alibi?" sneered Anastasia.

"Alibi?!" huffed Drucilla in righteous outrage. "We'll see about that!" Cinderella's two stepsisters took their quarrel to their mother, but she was anything but sympathetic.

"Don't bother me now," she said irritably. "Can't you see I'm busy? I have misplaced my glasses. Here, you two—help me look." And the three of them spent the next hour looking under cushions and into drawers and peering under furniture. Their efforts went unrewarded.

On the other side of the castle, the King was trying on a new dress uniform. He was about to admire himself in the mirror when he noticed that the jacket had a button missing.

"Summon the Grand Duke!" he roared. Cries of "Grand Duke!" echoed through the castle until they reached the Grand Duke himself.

When he appeared before the King, the Duke found his monarch pacing his royal carpet. "Yes, Your . . ." was all the poor man got out.

"It's about time!" said the King. "I'm surrounded by incompetents. Look at these buttons!"

"Why, Sire," replied the Duke, puzzled. "They're wonderful buttons—fit for a king."

They were indeed elegant buttons, but there were only four instead of five.

"Do you notice anything about them?" inquired the King.

"Well, Sire . . . " began the Duke, squinting.

"One is missing!" roared the King. "Are you blind?"

"As a matter of fact, Your Majesty," the Duke answered, "I am, a bit. You see I've mislaid my monocle, and I was just looking for it when . . . "

"Well, find it!" commanded the King. "Then FIND MY BUTTON!"

By this time the castle was in a proper uproar, and the commotion was making it impossible for Gus and Jaq to finish their naps. Jaq was mumbling something about "silly humans" when he saw Suzy Mouse hurrying toward his sunny corner, a cloud of worry on her brow.

"Oh, Jaq!" she cried. "You must help me. I can't find my silver thimble."

"Oh, thimble, shmimble. Do your sewing some other day and let me nap in peace," grumbled Jaq.

"Listen here, Jaq Mouse," replied Suzy. "Don't forget who makes the lemonade and cookies around here. You'd better find my thimble," she declared, stamping her tiny foot, "and you, Gus, had better help him! Or there'll be no more lemonade—and no more cookies!"

Suzy turned on her heel and marched away.

"Uh-oh," breathed Gus. "We'd better look for that thimble."

"Right, Gus-Gus. We're super sleuths. We'll find Suzy's thimble in no time."

They first asked all their friends for help. The mice carefully searched their dwellings, especially the lady mice, who knew the importance of thimbles, but no silver thimble did they find.

"I guess we'll have to search room by room," sighed Jaq. They began in the kitchen, which wasn't easy, what with dodging the kitchen maid's feet and the cook's broom. They searched the whole first floor of the castle, without luck—but not without incident.

In the parlor, where the maid had not yet removed the dishes from afternoon tea, Gus became so interested in searching for biscuit crumbs that he forgot all about looking for thimbles. Jaq, busily looking through the fringe on the parlor rugs, heard the sound of snoring from the tea table. He scampered up the table leg and there was his partner, tummy full of biscuit crumbs, finishing his afternoon nap on a napkin.

"Gus-Gus!" squeaked Jaq. "This is no time to loaf!" Gus awoke, thinking it must be dinner time. He had the good grace to be embarrassed as he followed Jaq to the second floor, where they

"Jaq!" squeaked Gus.

"Shush! Get me out of here!" came the frantic reply.

Gus grasped his friend's hand and heaved mightily. He freed Jaq—but he woke the cat!

"We're in for it now!" yelled Jaq, grabbing Gus and dashing for the door. Lucifer took a good swipe at them, but just missed, and both mice escaped.

"That was too close," gasped Jaq, leaning against a wall to catch his breath. "Let's put some more distance between us and the cat. We'll search the tower."

"But it's locked," protested Gus.

"We have to look everywhere," Jaq pointed out. "Remember what Suzy said about no more cookies and lemonade?"

The tower room hadn't been used in ages and was, in fact, kept locked. Jaq and Gus squeezed under the door.

"Boy, it's dusty in here!" sneezed Gus. "Nobody's been here in years. I don't think we'll find Suzy's thimble here."

Then, in one corner, they noticed a pile of objects that weren't so dusty. There were the emerald necklace and the ruby earring, the Grand Duke's monocle and the Stepmother's glasses, a shiny button from the King's new uniform and, on top of the pile, Suzy's precious thimble.

had no better success than they'd had on the first.

As the mice started for the third floor and the family bedrooms, Jaq cautioned, "Watch out for Lucifee. He's still a pretty sneaky cat." Lucifer, of course, enjoyed chasing a mouse now and then, just to keep in shape.

The last bedroom to be searched on the third floor belonged to Cinderella's stepmother. Gus was all for assuming that Suzy's thimble wasn't there, but Jaq insisted on a thorough search. He straightened his shoulders, plucked up his courage, and peeked inside. There, on a velvet cushion by the velvet-draped bed, was Lucifer, peacefully dreaming. The two mice tiptoed about, looking under the bed, behind the drapes, and between the cushions on the sofa.

Finally, they came to the cat's bed. "No, no, Jaq!" whispered Gus, pulling at his friend's arm.

"We may as well do this right," gulped Jaq, and he crept over to Lucifer's side. He was about to look under the cat's tail when Lucifer gave a snort and rolled over, pinning the unfortunate Jaq beneath him.

While the two mice were examining this hoard, a voice came from the direction of the tower window. "Hi ya, boys! Quite a haul, eh?" Down from the dusty sill hopped a crow.

"Who are you?" asked Jaq.

"Cedrick Crow's my name," replied the bird. "Treasure's my game!"

"You can't keep all these things," scolded Jaq. "They belong to the royal family."

"Oh, yes, I can," answered the crow. "Finders, keepers. Now, shoo, you two!"

"We're going to need help," said Jaq. And off they scampered to Cinderella's room. By hopping up and down and squeaking urgently, they persuaded her to follow them up to the tower.

When he saw Jaq and Gus, Cedrick was none too pleased. "Didn't I tell you guys to leave me alone?" he squawked. Then he noticed Cinderella.

"Why, hello, there," said Cinderella. "What a grand bird you are—and what lovely feathers!"

Now Cedrick was not a crow to resist flattery. He puffed out his feathers and strutted back and forth.

Cinderella pointed to the crow's hoard. "Those things belong to others. I'm sorry, but you'll have to return them."

Cedrick squawked in protest, but he felt himself weakening.

"Don't worry," soothed Cinderella. "Come with me." She gathered up the shiny objects, put them in her pocket, and down they all went to the first floor of the castle.

Cinderella stopped in front of a large door. When she'd opened it, Cedrick nearly swooned.

For the room to which she'd brought him was the royal treasure room, full of gold and jewels.

"Here, now," she said, setting the crow on the back of the royal counting chair. "I'm quite sure His Majesty will agree to a small bargain. You may make this room your home if you will agree to be its guard."

Cedrick was overcome, and he flapped his wings in excitement. So Anastasia got back her ruby earring, and Drucilla her emerald necklace. The Grand Duke and the Stepmother could both see again, and the King's new uniform shone once more with all five buttons.

And Suzy was so grateful to get her silver thimble back that she fixed *two* pitchers of lemonade and baked *two* batches of molasses cookies for Gus and Jaq—the *two* bravest mice in Cinderella's castle.

Question: The blue-gray area in the lower right corner shows the metropolitan area of the largest city on the west coast of the United States. What city is it?

Answer: Los Angeles. The triangular area in the upper right corner is the Mojave Desert. Red squares in the desert are irrigated farmland areas.

Question: The twisting, braided object at the top of the picture is a part of the longest river in South America. The red background is the tropical rain forest through which it flows. What is the name of the river?

Answer: The Amazon River. The river flowing from lower left to upper right is the Purus, a tributary of the Amazon. The white line in the lower right corner is a road cut through the rain forest.

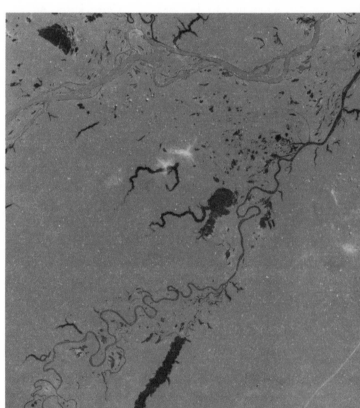

Question: The blue-gray area shows the largest city in the United States, with neighboring cities and suburbs. What is the name of this largest city?

Answer: New York City. The red areas within the city are trees and grass in the city parks.

WHAT ON EARTH. . .?

Two United States satellites, Landsat 1 and 2, are following a nearly circular orbit around the earth. From a height of 570 miles (917 kilometers) they send information that enables earth-based computers to assemble amazingly detailed pictures of the earth, like those you see here. These pictures are being used by many countries around the world to make accurate maps, plan transportation routes, check on floods, trace sea ice, monitor air pollution, and do many other jobs in surveying the earth and its resources.

Because of the way the pictures are produced, they usually have false colors—the colors are not "actual" colors of the earth as seen from a spacecraft. So remember as you look at the pictures on these pages: grass and trees are seen as red; clear deep water is black; shallow water is blue; and cities are blue-gray. Now, can you tell what on earth you are seeing in these pictures?

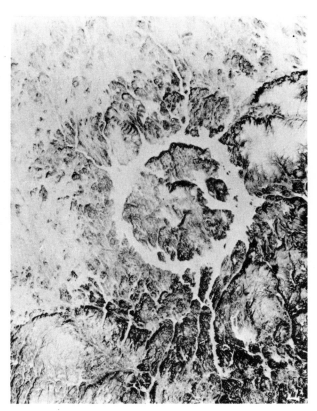

Question: Imagine a line passing between the two small islands near the center of the picture. That line forms the boundary between two great countries on two continents. The line also separates Monday from Tuesday. What is the line called? Which countries and which continents does it separate?

Answer: The line is the International Date Line, which is also the boundary between Siberia in the Soviet Union (*left*) and Alaska in the United States (*right*). The continents are Asia and North America.

Question: The circular object is in east central Quebec, in Canada. It is 41 miles (66 kilometers) in diameter. What is the object? What are the branchlike structures around it?

Answer: This is Lake Manicouagan, partly frozen over. The branching objects are frozen streams. The lake fills a depression that may have resulted from the explosion of a gigantic meteor, or it may be the remains of an ancient volcanic cone.

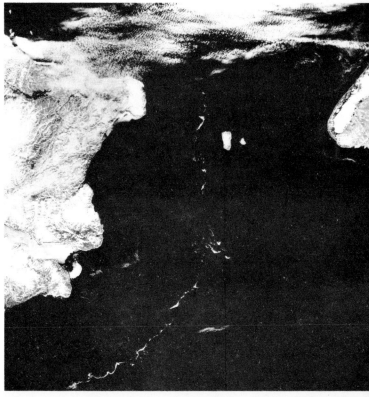

THE POLAR BEAR EXPRESS

"All aboard!" A conductor sings out the words as late arrivals scurry on board the Ontario Northland diesel train. It's eight o'clock on a sunny summer morning, and we're about to take a trip on a very special train—the Polar Bear Express.

Every day except Friday, from mid-June to early September, the Polar Bear Express pulls out of Cochrane, in Canada's province of Ontario. Its destination is Moosonee, a small frontier town 186 miles (300 kilometers) to the north, at the southern tip of James Bay.

So try to get a seat next to a window. We're on our way to one of the last great wilderness frontiers of North America. The Polar Bear Express is taking us on an adventure-filled journey—a journey through a region of scenic splendor, where the romance of history blends with the modern wonders of today.

With a lurch, the train starts its 4½-hour run, twisting and turning through thick woodlands. Soon we get our first glimpse of the swift-flowing waters of the mighty Abitibi River. We are traveling along a route used by French troops under Chevalier de Troyes nearly 300 years ago. Back in 1686, De Troyes and his men braved the wilderness to attack and capture the British Hudson's Bay Company post (called Moose Factory) on an island near James Bay.

Soon we'll be passing places with such colorful names as Red Sucker—where Indians still trap beaver and other animals—Big Jaw Bone River, and Otter Rapids. There's lots to dazzle the eyes—moose loping in the wild; shimmering lakes; high waterfalls; giant dams and modern power plants. See that unusual-looking bridge? That's called an "upside-down" bridge. (It looks like an upside-down suspension bridge.) It's built that way to allow ice to pass underneath during the spring thaw.

If you get tired of looking out of the window, you might walk back to the special museum car. Here you will find fascinating exhibits tracing the history of northern Ontario. You might also look around at the people you are traveling with. Mixed in with the tourists, there are some Cree Indians. A few have brought canoes with them, so that when they leave the train, they can paddle up the river to their homes.

We're now coming into Moosonee—the "gateway to the Arctic." Some of our fellow passengers may be prospectors or geologists. They will head for the waterfront to board ships and bush planes that will take them to the far north. Beyond Moosonee, Canada's vast woodlands and tundra stretch nearly 2,000 miles (3,300 kilometers) to the Arctic Circle. This is the land of polar bears and Eskimos. It's also where geologists and prospectors are searching for gold, silver, and other valuable minerals.

While the scientists and prospectors go their way, we can take a canoe trip to Moose Factory Island. In 1673, the British set up a fur trading post there, and Moose Factory became the first English-speaking settlement in Ontario. Today, fur trading goes on, just as it has for the past 300 years.

There, too, we can wander around the Centennial Park Museum and view relics of the past. We can also visit the Indian residential school, where more than 200 Indian children go. And we can step into century-old St. Thomas' Church, with its beaded moose-hide altar cloths.

The hours slip by, and soon it is time to get back on the train for the return trip. We'll carry back with us the memory of a wonderful journey on the fabled Polar Bear Express.

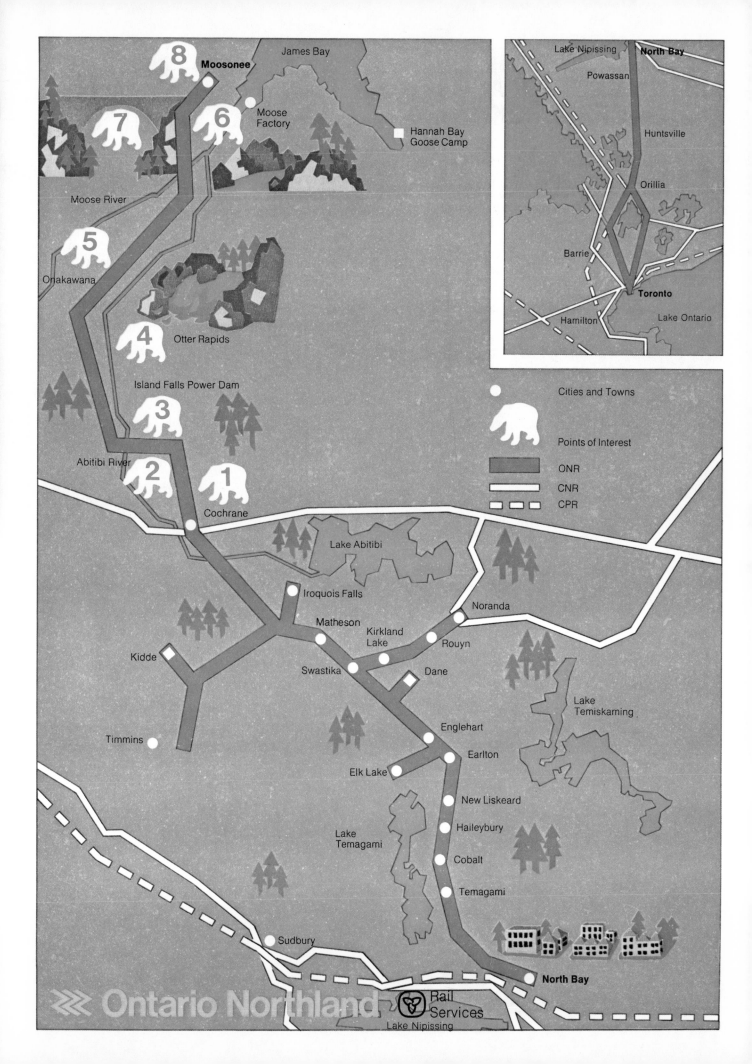

Moosonee

James Bay

Moose Factory

Hannah Bay Goose Camp

Moose River

Onakawana

Otter Rapids

Island Falls Power Dam

Abitibi River

Cochrane

Lake Abitibi

Iroquois Falls

Matheson

Kirkland Lake

Kidde

Swastika

Dane

Noranda

Rouyn

Timmins

Englehart

Elk Lake

Earlton

Lake Temiskaming

New Liskeard

Haileybury

Lake Temagami

Cobalt

Temagami

Sudbury

North Bay

Lake Nipissing

≫≫ Ontario Northland Rail Services

Lake Nipissing

North Bay

Powassan

Huntsville

Orillia

Barrie

Toronto

Hamilton

Lake Ontario

Cities and Towns

Points of Interest

ONR

CNR

CPR

EMBROIDER A POCKETBOOK

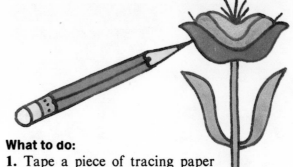

What to use:

2 squares of felt (for front and back
of pocketbook, each about the
size shown in the finished picture on page 137)
1 square of a different-colored felt (for handle)
pencil
tracing paper
scissors
straight pins
embroidery needle
6-strand embroidery floss (7 colors)
tape

What to do:

1. Tape a piece of tracing paper over the picture on page 137. Trace the pocketbook and all the designs on it. Remove tracing paper. Now take a soft lead pencil and vigorously rub it over the back of the tracing paper. Pin the paper, penciled side down, over one felt pocketbook square. Trace over the lines on the paper. Remove paper. The black lines on the felt are the designs that you will embroider.

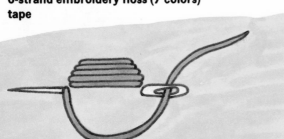

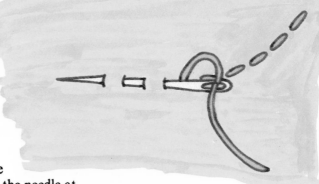

2. Here are two kinds of stitches. **Satin stitch:** Starting from the wrong side of the felt, bring the needle up at one edge of a design to be embroidered. Now insert the needle at the opposite edge, and return to the starting edge by carrying the thread underneath the felt. Make stitches parallel and close together. **Running stitch:** Insert the needle in and out of the felt, making even stitches.

3. Embroider all the designs. Then, take your scissors and cut all around the outside edges of the pocketbook. This is the front. Pin it to the other square of pocketbook felt, cut around it, and you will have the back.

4. Pin the front and back together. Using the running stitch, sew around the outline of the pocketbook leaving scalloped edge open (as shown in the finished picture).

5. Trace the handle from the finished picture onto tracing paper. Pin tracing to your remaining square of felt and cut out the handle. Place the handle inside the top of your two pocketbook pieces and fasten with a few stitches.

THE MYSTERY OF THE MONARCHS

For almost forty years, Fred Urquhart tried to solve a mystery. He wasn't alone. Thousands of people helped him track his subject. Reports from the field poured in—the subject was seen in Florida, in Tennessee, in Texas.

Fred Urquhart is a professor of zoology at Scarborough College in Toronto, Canada. His subject is the monarch butterfly.

The delicate black and orange monarch is a common summer sight where Urquhart lives. It is familiar to most people who live in Canada and the northern United States. Go into a garden or a field and you are almost certain to see a monarch or two enjoying the flowers and the warm sun.

Monarch butterflies gather in dense, hanging clusters on the branches of trees.

But as the night grows longer and cooler, and autumn comes, the monarchs leave their summer homes. Like many birds and other animals, but unlike most butterflies, they migrate to a warmer place for the winter.

Those that summer in western parts of Canada and the United States fly to central and southern California. There, they gather in dense, hanging clusters on the branches of pine, oak, cypress, and eucalyptus trees.

And those that summer in the eastern parts —well, no one could discover where they went. Urquhart worked hard to solve this mystery. But the trail always seemed to disappear in Texas, on the Mexican border.

Urquhart's wife wrote to Mexican newspapers, asking people to write if they saw monarchs. This eventually led to a phone call in January, 1975, from a resident of Mexico City, who believed the colony of monarchs had been found.

Urquhart and his wife journeyed to the Sierra Madre mountains in south central Mexico. And there, on a remote mountainside, they saw millions and millions of monarch butterflies hanging from the trees.

"I gazed in amazement at the sight," wrote Urquhart. "They clung in tightly packed masses to every branch and trunk.... They swirled through the air like autumn leaves and carpeted the ground.... Unbelievable! What a glorious, incredible sight!"

Scientists would like to keep the location of the Mexican mountainside a secret. They don't want it turned into a tourist attraction. They also want to prevent local farmers from collecting the butterflies, which are a rich source of protein, to use as cattle food.

And so, a mystery has been solved. But another, perhaps more interesting mystery remains unsolved. How do the monarchs know where to go? Monarch butterflies live less than a year. Those that flew south last fall will die this spring or summer. A new generation of monarchs, hatched from eggs laid this year, will head south in the fall. How do these monarchs—who have never before flown south— know where to go? How do they know about that remote mountainside in Mexico, some 3,000 miles (5,000 kilometers) away?

A TREE HOUSE MAZE

Oh, bother! Pooh's ladder is broken, and now he'll have to find another way to get to the hunny in his tree house. Can you help him? Start at the arrow at the bottom of the tree and work your way up to the door. HINT: Poor Pooh even has to go through the leaves. (Look on page 126 for the answer.)

These scenes illustrate some of the exciting adventures in Daniel Defoe's *Robinson Crusoe.*

ROBINSON CRUSOE'S ISLAND

In the Pacific Ocean, about 400 miles (650 kilometers) west of Valparaiso, Chile, there is a small island that has become famous throughout the world. It is an island of magnificent beauty. Parts of it are barren rock and jagged vertical cliffs, while other parts are covered with lush greenery. The peak of the island's highest mountain is almost always hidden by churning clouds. They leap and dive against the broad face of the mountain, and then rush off to pour rain upon nearby valleys.

The island is one of a group known as the Juan Fernández Islands, named for their discoverer. But this island has become better known as Robinson Crusoe's island. For it was here that Alexander Selkirk, a sailor from Scotland, lived completely alone for four years and four months. Selkirk's experience would probably have been forgotten if Daniel Defoe had not used it as the basis for *Robinson Crusoe,* one of the world's most famous books. Because of the great popularity of *Robinson Crusoe,* Selkirk's little island has become famous too.

▶ **SELKIRK'S STORY**

The island was discovered about 1563 by Juan Fernández, a Spanish navigator, who came upon it by accident. He settled there for a while, stocking the island with goats and pigs. However, Fernández' attempts at agriculture failed, and he soon left.

Other early settlers, the Jesuits, were also unsuccessful, and the island remained uninhabited. But it became a refuge for bands of English pirates, who found it a perfect hiding place before and after their raids. From the 16th to the 18th century, the island was a haven for many a pirate ship.

Occasionally, other ships stopped there too, but only for a short time. One of these ships was the *Cinque Ports,* an English galley that came by in October, 1704, and put off an unhappy sailor named Alexander Selkirk. Selkirk, it seemed, had quarreled with his captain. Rather than put up with the captain any longer, Selkirk asked to be put ashore. His request was granted.

Selkirk, then 28 years old, landed with the most basic of equipment—a change of clothes and two blankets; an iron saucepan and a drinking jar; an ax, a knife, a cutlass, a pistol, and a musket; and a pound of gunpowder and a bag of tobacco. He also had his Bible.

Living alone made Selkirk learn how to keep alive with nothing more than his own inventiveness and skill. He had to be a woodcutter and carpenter; a hunter, butcher, and cook; a tailor and a launderer. His many tasks probably kept him from going mad with loneliness. Yet one can imagine the terrifying hours that he must have lived through at the beginning, when the night and the ocean wrapped the island in a vast, silent darkness.

Early in his stay on the island, Selkirk spotted goats climbing nimbly among the hills and cliffs. These animals were probably the descendants of the first goats brought there by the discoverer Fernández. They provided Selkirk with food, clothing, shelter, and amazingly enough, companionship.

Selkirk built a small hut of logs and sticks. He covered the roof and sides with the hides of goats he had shot with his musket. For food, he ate their meat. But Selkirk soon ran out of gunpowder, and so his musket was useless. He then had no choice but to try to catch the goats with his bare hands.

How could a lone man catch one of those agile creatures with his bare hands? Selkirk must have been a dazzling gymnast, for only a fine athlete could have done what he did: leaping like an acrobat along the edges of cliffs, he caught the goats on the run!

One time he slipped, and rolled with his catch down a steep cliff. He blacked out. When he revived, he discovered that the little goat lay dead beneath him—like a pillow that had been placed by luck to break his fall and save his life. This accident gave him the idea of having goats live with him. To keep them from running away, he built a stockade around his hut. In that corral, the goats became tame. They reproduced, and the kids became his friends and companions. He taught them to dance and to leap, and when he went walking they followed him about.

Like anyone who must survive in the wilderness, Selkirk had to rely more on cleverness than on physical strength. He made fire by rubbing dry sticks together. He scraped sea

salt from the hollows of rocks, where it had collected from dried-up seawater. For light he burned oil from sea lions, which he had killed with a club. In the rain-soaked valleys, he found wild fruits and vegetables. He fished from the beach with a net made of goat intestines. And when his clothing finally wore out, he made himself an outfit of goatskin. He sewed it with strands of rawhide, using a thinned nail as a needle.

And so this remarkable man got used to his solitary life. His beard grew long and wild. His feet grew hard from walking barefoot on the rough forest floor. He did not know if he would ever see another human again. And afraid that he might lose the ability to speak, he talked to himself or read the Bible aloud. In time, Selkirk became an "island man." He later said, "Nowhere could I be as happy again as I was on my island."

Humans are called "social animals"—they enjoy and need the company of other people. Was Selkirk different? Perhaps. But day after day, he climbed a mountain to watch the sea in hope of spotting a sail. Once he spied a ship flying the flag of France. He signaled to it, but either the sailors did not see him or they decided to ignore him. Another time, a Spanish ship anchored offshore. Unfortunately, Spain and England were enemies at the time. Selkirk was seen and chased like a wild beast. He had

Above: Selkirk, the real-life model for the fictional Crusoe. Below: Selkirk greets the captain of the *Duke*.

to flee to the forest and hide in the top of a tree.

From Selkirk's experiences, we can see that people can learn to live under the most difficult circumstances. There is no doubt that Selkirk could have survived for years and years. He did not later mention ever having been sad or bored. So far as is known, he was never sick in the four years and four months he spent on the island. He probably came to feel that time did not exist; he lived alone with the island, the sea, and the sky. And perhaps there were times when he actually stopped caring if he would ever be rescued.

In February, 1709, an English ship, the *Duke*, reached the island. The captain found Selkirk on the beach, clothed in skins and accompanied by his goats. The call of human society was too strong to resist. Selkirk went on board the *Duke* and left his island forever. Later he married and made his home in England. Ever the seagoing man, he went to sea again, with the rank of master's mate. It is possible that Selkirk met Daniel Defoe in Bristol and told the author about his adventures. *Robinson Crusoe* was published in 1719, just two years before Selkirk died. Selkirk read the book and protested that his island had been changed into a Caribbean isle with parrots! Nevertheless, his island became known as Robinson Crusoe's island.

▶HIS ISLAND LIVES ON

One cannot blame Selkirk for protesting. Why change such a beautiful island? The climate ranges between temperate and subtropical. Showers fall in midsummer, and the loveliness of autumn is without equal. The blue-green waters surrounding the island are filled with fish. If there really is a paradise on earth, perhaps this is it.

After Selkirk left, the island remained uninhabited for many years. Sailors and soldiers came and went. The island belonged to Spain until 1818. In that year, the island passed into the hands of the newly independent country of Chile. And as the years went by, settlers came to the island and stayed.

Today, about seven hundred people live on Robinson Crusoe's island. The little town of San Juan Bautista sits on Cumberland Bay, one of the island's natural harbors. This lively town spreads among groves and orchards on a hill backed by steep mountains. In the town live fishermen, farmers, officials, and even some modern Robinson Crusoes who are looking for the solitary joy that Selkirk knew. Many tourists also come each year, drawn by the island's rich history and legendary beauty. And anyone who sees this island will understand the sorrow of Selkirk's long-ago cry:

"Oh, my beloved island, I wish I had never left thee!"

December 24, 1822: Dr. Clement Clarke Moore reads "A Visit from St. Nicholas" to his children.

THE MAN WHO INVENTED SANTA CLAUS

St. Nicholas of Myra is a patron saint of Russia. He has also been one of the patron saints of children for centuries. Legend has it that St. Nicholas brings gifts to good children on his day, December 6. There are many other legends about him too. But Santa Claus, as most North Americans have come to know St. Nicholas, was born on December 24, 1822. It was on that frosty Christmas Eve that Dr. Clement Clarke Moore, a scholar and part-time poet, penned the lines of the immortal poem "A Visit from St. Nicholas." Moore turned St. Nicholas into "jolly St. Nick," a plump, happy-go-lucky elf with a sleigh full of toys and eight prancing reindeer, and sent him flying over hill and dale to keep alive the spirit of giving. And so a new St. Nicholas legend came to be.

Here is a dramatized account of how Dr. Moore created Santa Claus.

It was a cold evening and the ground was covered with snow. Dr. Moore was on his way home to his estate in what is now the Chelsea section of New York City. He had just delivered Christmas presents to friends in Greenwich Village. Driving his sleigh was an old Dutch handyman named Peter, whose weather-beaten face seemed always to wear a smile, and who could be counted upon for a cheerful remark when the world seemed gloomiest.

Suddenly, the 43-year-old professor remembered that he had promised his children a poem as an extra Christmas present. For although he was a scholar by profession, he often wrote light verse for his family's amusement.

"By heaven, I'd nearly forgotten about that," Dr. Moore muttered to himself as old Peter, silhouetted in the moonlight, flicked his whip to spur on the horses. Dr. Moore racked his brain for an idea, turning over in his mind many possible lines of verse. But none seemed just right. Suddenly his eye fell on Peter's face, illuminated by the soft beams of the moon. The handyman's cherubic features, the pipe clenched firmly between his teeth, and the stocking cap pulled tightly over his head gave Dr. Moore an inspiration.

When they arrived home, the professor hurried to his study. "But dinner will be ready shortly," his wife protested. "Yes, yes, I know," Dr. Moore replied. "Just give me a few minutes. I have something important to do."

Alone at his desk, he began to write. The words flowed easily as his quill pen made scratchy sounds on the yellow manuscript paper. "Twas the night before Christmas," he began, "when all through the house, not a creature was stirring, not even a mouse . . ."

"Ah yes, that's exactly right," the professor announced to himself, pleased with his efforts. Quickly, he continued:

> The stockings were hung by the
>   chimney with care
> In hopes that St. Nicholas soon
>   would be there;
> The children were nestled all snug
>   in their beds,
> While visions of sugar-plums danced
>   in their heads;

By the time the family was seated at the dinner table, Dr. Moore had completed all 58 lines of his poem. After dinner he and his wife and children gathered around the fireplace for their traditional singing of Christmas carols. But the children had not forgotten their father's promise.

"You said you would give us a Christmas poem," they chorused, pulling at the sleeves of his frock coat.

At first, Dr. Moore pretended to have forgotten. "A poem? Was I supposed to write a poem?" he asked, a slight smile on his face. Then, as his children looked on with obvious disappointment, he fumbled through his pockets as if trying to find something he had misplaced. "Wait a minute!" he announced triumphantly. "Here's something."

And with a flourish, he pulled out the long yellow sheets containing the newly written verses.

While his children sat at his feet, Dr. Moore began to read. From the moment he spoke the opening lines, the youngsters were captivated.

They listened attentively as he declared: "The moon, on the breast of the new-fallen snow, gave the lustre of mid-day to objects below. When what to my wondering eyes should appear, but a miniature sleigh, and eight tiny rein-deer. With a little old driver, so lively and quick, I knew in a moment it must be St. Nick."

While the children beamed, Dr. Moore continued, describing how Santa drove his sleigh over the roofs of the buildings and called his reindeer by name: "Now, *Dasher!* now, *Dancer!* now, *Prancer* and *Vixen!* On, *Comet!* on, *Cupid!* on, *Donder* and *Blitzen!*" But it was when the professor read the lines describing the old fellow in detail, and telling how he came down the chimney "with a bound," that the eyes of his children widened in rapture:

> He was dressed all in fur, from his
>   head to his foot,
> And his clothes were all tarnished
>   with ashes and soot;
> A bundle of toys he had flung on his
>   back,
> And he looked like a peddler just
>   opening his pack.
> His eyes—how they twinkled! his
>   dimples, how merry!
> His cheeks were like roses, his nose
>   like a cherry!

His droll little mouth was drawn up
   like a bow,
And the beard on his chin was as
   white as the snow;
The stump of a pipe he held tight in
   his teeth,
And the smoke, it encircled his head
   like a wreath;
He had a broad face and a round little
   belly
That shook, when he laughed, like a bowl
   full of jelly.
He was chubby and plump, a right jolly old
   elf,
And I laughed when I saw him, in spite
   of myself;

Dr. Moore's children loved the poem so much that they immediately began to memorize the lines. But the professor himself thought little of it; to him it was just a funny story in verse. Never dreaming of its future popularity, or even of having it published, he shoved it into a desk drawer and forgot all about it.

Some months later, a family acquaintance, Harriet Butler of Troy, New York, visited the Moores. Dr. Moore read the poem aloud while they were having tea. Miss Butler was very much taken by the verses and asked permission to make copies. Later she sent one of them to her local newspaper, the Troy *Sentinel,* but failed to mention the author's name.

The Troy newspaper happily published the "anonymous" poem just before Christmas in 1823, noting in its columns: "We know not to whom we are indebted for the following description of the unwearied patron of children . . . but from whomsoever it may come, we give thanks for it."

For years afterward, the poem was often published by newspapers and magazines during the Yuletide season—but without any credit being given to Dr. Moore. In 1830 a wood engraver named Myron King produced the first illustration of St. Nick and his eight reindeer—just as they were described in "A Visit from St. Nicholas." (Santa remained a tiny elf for nearly 40 years. Only in the 1860's did he take his present-day shape of a plump gentleman of normal height, dressed in a red, fur-trimmed suit. And this was due to the American political cartoonist Thomas Nast, who drew Santa that way during the American Civil War.)

As for Dr. Moore, he finally got the credit due him when a collection of verse entitled *The New York Book of Poetry* carried the poem with his name on it in 1837. In 1844 the professor included it in one of his own books, but made it a point to note that he considered it of no more significance than "a good, honest, hearty laugh."

Certainly Dr. Moore never imagined that this little verse would eclipse all his scholarly writings on the Bible and Classical literature. And yet this is exactly what happened. Today not even the most serious scholars are more than vaguely acquainted with Dr. Moore's academic works; but millions of people throughout the world have read and been delighted by "A Visit from St. Nicholas."

The poem has now been reprinted many thousands of times, in dozens of languages. And each year at Columbia University there is a Christmas event known as the Lighting of the Yule Log. It is traditional at this ceremony to read the poem by Dr. Moore, who graduated from Columbia in 1798 at the head of his class and later became a member of its Board of Trustees.

Despite the immense popularity of his poem, Dr. Moore never earned a single penny from it. He probably would have refused the money anyway, for he was a man of independent means who preferred giving to receiving. In fact, Clement Clarke Moore was very much like the Santa Claus he wrote about—a man who quietly went about the job of bringing joy to others, and who was amply rewarded by the happiness he left in his wake. So Professor Moore might well have been describing himself in the closing lines of his time-honored poem:

He spoke not a word, but went straight
   to his work,
And he filled all the stockings; then
   turned with a jerk,
And laying a finger aside of his nose,
And giving a nod, up the chimney he
   rose.
He sprang to his sleigh, to his team
   gave a whistle,
And away they all flew like the down
   of a thistle;
But I heard him exclaim, ere he drove
   out of sight,
"HAPPY CHRISTMAS TO ALL,
AND TO ALL A GOOD-NIGHT!"

MOPEDS

Michael Patterson drives a special kind of vehicle—it goes 180 miles on one gallon of gas (77 kilometers on one liter)! He's saving money on gas, he's saving energy, and he's saving our environment by polluting it less. Michael is one of the many people who have discovered mopeds (pronounced MO-ped). The moped—short for "motor plus pedals"—is a motorized bicycle.

For many years, millions of Europeans and Asians have been using mopeds as their basic form of transportation. But these vehicles have only recently become popular in North America. Now, executives are riding them to work. Housewives are using them to go shopping. Students are using them to get to school. (Anyone who is at least 16 years old—14 in some areas—may ride one.) And besides being an energy-saving form of transportation, mopeds are fun to ride.

Most mopeds weigh about 90 to 100 pounds (40 to 50 kilograms). The engine runs on gasoline mixed with a little motor oil. They have automatic transmission, which means the rider doesn't have to shift gears. A moped, which costs about $300 to $600, comes with headlight and taillight, as well as other safety equipment. All kinds of accessories can also be bought: rearview mirrors, baskets and saddlebags, even a carrier that attaches the moped to the rear bumper of a car.

It takes just a few minutes to learn to operate a moped. You start the engine by pedaling. Once it is running, you don't do any more pedaling—unless you want to. (On a steep hill, you may have to pedal to help the engine.) To stop, you use the hand brakes.

Mopeds are designed for short-distance trips. You can ride them at speeds of about 17 to 25 miles per hour (27 to 40 kilometers per hour), depending on the laws in your area. But you cannot ride them on limited-access highways, such as freeways and thruways.

Some Moped Tips. Before buying one, find out about the laws that apply to mopeds in your area. In some states and Canadian provinces, your moped must be licensed, registered, or insured, and you must wear a helmet; in other areas, a moped is considered a kind of bicycle, and there are few laws. When you ride a moped, follow the same safety rules that you would if riding a bicycle. Ride on the right side of the road, single file. Use hand signals when turning. At night, use lights. Don't ride your moped on the sidewalk. Park your moped as you would a bike, and use a high-security lock.

Happy mopeding!

A giant kite skin is stretched over a bamboo frame.

GUATEMALA'S FLYING MESSENGERS

Santiago Sacatepéquez is a small Cakchiquel Indian village in Guatemala. It is spread across a gentle hillside in the central highlands, a few miles from Guatemala City, the capital. Santiago, like many another Guatemalan village, is distinguished mainly by the costume of its women. This consists of a *huipil*, or blouse, woven on the backstrap loom, thickly brocaded with red geometrical patterns; and a dark-blue skirt held in place by a multicolored sash. But since many Guatemalan villages have their own special costumes, visitors would not be expected to flock to Santiago just to see the beautiful *huipils*. But they do flock there for something else: a colorful ceremony held every year on November 1, All Saints' Day. (All Saints' Day is a Christian religious holiday honoring the saints, both known and unknown.)

Beginning in early September of each year, for no one knows how many generations, the young men of the village have devoted their spare time and energies to an art nearly as complicated and demanding as the weaving of the women's *huipils*. It is the art of kite making—but these are very special kites used for a very special purpose.

First a small circle of thin colored paper is placed on the floor. Then concentric rings, each with its own distinct design, are pasted around it, one after another. The kite grows outward, expanding, until it is soon too large to be fully unfolded inside the small Indian house.

The average kite skin measures 5 yards (4.5 meters) across; the biggest may be more than 30 feet (9 meters). As many as ten men work on each kite, and it takes six to eight weeks to complete one—about the same amount of time required for a woman to weave a *huipil*. But the kites will last a single afternoon, whereas the *huipil* is made to last for years.

On the morning of November 1, the women of Santiago go to the graveyard on a hillside outside of the town. There they scatter petals of wild marigold over the tombs and bare-

The finished kites are poised upright like huge shields, awaiting a strong gust of wind.

earth mounds. The people of the village call these flowers *flores de muerto* ("flowers of the dead"). Back in the village, in the courtyards of the little adobe houses, the men spend the morning stretching their giant kite skins over bamboo frames. Early in the afternoon, when breezes begin to blow over the hills, they carry the kites to the graveyard and poise them upright, like huge shields, along a fence at its downhill end. With their guy lines attached, taut, the pilots wait uphill for a westward gust of wind strong enough to take their craft aloft.

The kites are messages for the dead. Greetings. Tokens of remembrance, like the marigolds. Some kites never lift more than a few feet off the ground. Others catch strong breezes and rise high above the mountains. But these too soon come down. Some break up in the air, or, when the wind slackens, they tilt and nose-dive into the groves and cornfields of the valley below. When each has been damaged beyond repair, its makers rip off the paper skin and set it afire, saving only the bamboo poles to use again the following year. And so this ancient tradition—flying messengers for the dead—lives on.

Up, up, and away—the flying messengers for the dead are carried aloft.

DISCOVERING YOUR ROOTS

It's a fact of life—you have two parents, four grandparents, eight great-grandparents, sixteen great-great-grandparents . . . and so on, back to the very beginnings of human existence. You probably know who your parents and grandparents are and where they came from. But who were your great-great-grandparents? Who were your ancestors in the 17th or 18th or 19th centuries? Where did they live? How did you get here if they lived there?

These are just a few of the many questions that people everywhere have begun more and more to ask themselves. They are searching for their "roots"—for the ancestors and heritage from which they descended.

By studying family records and following other leads, some people have been able to

Alex Haley (left) wrote the dramatic book Roots. It was made into a popular TV series with LeVar Burton as Kunta Kinte (below).

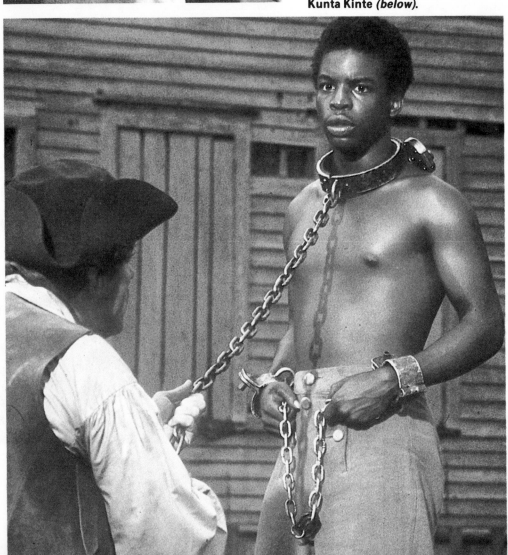

trace their families back hundreds of years. Most often a lot of work is involved. And finding the actual proof that shows that a particular person is really one of your ancestors is like solving a real-life mystery or a very difficult puzzle.

▶ ONE MAN'S SEARCH

Interest in family history greatly increased in 1977, thanks in large part to an American writer named Alex Haley. His book, *Roots,* told the story of Haley's nine-year-search for his family's origins. He began his search with stories that had been told to him by his grandmother in Tennessee. She had spoken of their ancestor, "the African," who left his village one day to cut wood to make himself a drum. While he was away from the village, he was captured by slave traders and shipped to the United States.

Haley's search for this ancestor took him to libraries and courthouses. It took him to London, where he studied the records of slave ships. It took him to a tiny village in Africa. There he spoke with an old man who knew the history of the village, and who told Haley about Kunta Kinte, the boy who had been captured while cutting wood—and who Haley believed was his ancestor.

Haley's dramatic book was made into an eight-part television series. It was watched by millions of Americans. (Some 80,000,000 people watched the last episode, the largest television audience in history.)

The book and the TV series inspired many people to hunt for their own roots. They enrolled in special courses given by local colleges and genealogical societies. They bought some of the many books that describe how to go about searching for one's ancestors. And they wrote or went to libraries and other places that could be of help. For example, the National Archives in Washington, D.C., received 758 inquiries in its family history services the week before the "Roots" series was televised, and then after the broadcasts, averaged 2,344 inquiries a week.

▶ WHERE TO LOOK

If you decide to search for your own roots, start at home. Talk to your relatives, especially the older ones. Ask for facts: birth dates, names of parents, names of places where they lived,

and so on. It is a good idea to prepare a fact sheet for each relative. It might look something like this:

MY ANCESTORS

Name of Person _____
Relation to Me _____
Birth Date _____ Place _____
Father's Name _____
Mother's Name _____
Brothers' and Sisters' Names _____

_____

Schools Attended _____

_____

Occupations _____

_____

_____

Where He/She Lived _____

_____

Spouse's Name _____
Marriage Date _____ Place _____
Children: Number _____

Name	Birth Date
_____	_____
_____	_____
_____	_____

You probably won't be able to fill in all the blanks on the fact sheet right away because you won't have all the information. But start a sheet even if all you know is the person's name. That makes him or her "real" to you. And as you go back several generations, your number of ancestors will quickly increase, causing confusion if you don't have a good system for recording information. (If you could trace your family back to the year 1600, you would be involved with about 65,000 ancestors!)

Also write down the stories that your relatives tell you—of what school was like, the games they played, the pets they had, the way they were affected by wars or elections or any other big events. You will discover that your relatives and ancestors have done many inter-

esting things. Perhaps some were famous— or infamous. One woman discovered that one of her ancestors was thought to have been a witch, and was burned at the stake in Salem, Massachusetts.

Some relatives may live far away. Perhaps you have never even met them. Write to them. Describe your project and ask for their help. Send along copies of your fact sheet and ask them to fill one out for each relative that they know of.

Ask your parents and relatives for family mementos: picture albums, family Bibles, diaries, letters, passports, birth and death certificates, marriage licenses. These things are often buried in attics or cellars, almost totally forgotten. It will take some gentle nudging on your part to get people to remember where they stored these things. But such papers can be very helpful. One woman found a letter that mentioned an uncle she didn't know existed, and a piece of property that everyone had forgotten about.

After you have gathered as much information as possible from your family, you are ready to check public records. This is where tracing ancestors begins to get especially difficult. But remember, you are a detective. And as any police detective would tell you, there's a lot of dull work involved both in the hunt for clues and in following up on the clues once you have them.

Public records include such things as land deeds, census records, wills, and military records. If, for example, you know that a great-great-grandfather settled in Sherman County, Kansas, in 1860, you could check county and town records to learn exactly where and when your ancestor bought land, what he paid for it, and how long he had it.

Churches and graveyards are also excellent sources of information. Churches have records of baptisms and marriages. Tombstones give birth and death dates, and often indicate family relationships or provide other information. This one tells us something of how a man died:

> This is the grave of Mike O'Day
> Who died maintaining his right of way.
> His right was clear, his will was strong,
> But he's just as dead as if he'd been wrong.

Public libraries have many books that tell about how to trace your roots. And some of the larger libraries have collections of old census records, newspapers, and other items that may help you.

There are also many historical societies, genealogical societies, and other groups that have collections and libraries that are devoted to the subject. One of the best of these is the central library of the Mormon Church in Salt Lake City, which has about 60,000,000 names on record, including both Mormons and non-Mormons.

Even telephone books can be helpful. One man who has an uncommon last name always checks telephone books in places he visits. If someone with the same last name is listed, the man writes or telephones the person to find out if they might be related.

▶ SEEING FOR YOURSELF

The information that you gather will become even more meaningful if you can visit the places where your ancestors lived. One young woman went to Czechoslovakia. There, in the city of Prague, she saw the house where her father's family had lived. She visited the church where her father had worshiped as a young boy, and she visited the hardware store where he had worked before leaving Czechoslovakia for America.

Traveling is not always an easy thing to do. It involves both time and money. But travel may be necessary to trace some of your ancestors. Knowing the language spoken by your ancestors is also helpful.

Occasionally, you will come to what seems to be a dead end. Perhaps records were lost or burned. For example, a big fire in Chicago destroyed almost all the city and county records up to 1872. Or people may have changed their names—or immigration officials changed them for them. Slaves were often given their owner's names. Names on official records may be misspelled.

But the problems will seem unimportant when compared with the joy you will feel as you learn about your family and how it survived and grew through one century after another. Tracing your roots gives history a sense of personal importance. And it tells you about yourself. As Alex Haley said, "We are what we are because of those who went before us."

JENNY TESAR
Consultant, Curriculum Concepts, Inc.

THE LONG AND THE SHORT OF IT

In Australia, an earthworm was found that was about 13 feet (400 centimeters) long. Even the tallest pro basketball player isn't that long!

At the other end of the scale is a worm that you would need a microscope to see. You would need more than 500 of these worms placed end to end to equal 1 inch (2.5 centimeters). How many would you need to equal that very long Australian worm? Nearly 80,000!

Here are some other very, very big and very, very small animals. We won't say they are world records—who knows what *you* will find the next time you go for a walk.

▶MAMMALS

The biggest mammal is the blue whale. It is not uncommon to find some that are 100 feet (30.5 meters) long and weigh 130 tons.

The smallest mammal is a pygmy shrew that lives in Africa. Its length, including its tail, is less than 2¼ inches (5.5 centimeters). It weighs under an ounce (about 2 grams).

Rodents

The capybara of South America is the biggest. Its head and body may be 4½ feet (135 centimeters) long, and it weighs about 175 pounds (80 kilograms). Sometimes called a water pig, because it spends most of its time in the water, it looks like a giant guinea pig.

The smallest rodent is the Old World harvest mouse. It is about 5 inches (12.5 centimeters) long, including its tail, and weighs only a fraction of an ounce (about 4 grams).

Dogs

The heaviest breed is the St. Bernard—one weighed 295 pounds (134 kilograms).

The smallest breed of dog is the Chihuahua —some weigh only a pound (.5 kilogram). They may be tiny, but this doesn't stop them from barking at St. Bernards!

▶SNAKES

The anaconda of South America is the longest. But it is probably not as long as rumored. Though people have reported seeing anacondas as long as 120 feet (37 meters), some of the largest ever measured were about 35 feet (11 meters) long. But that's big enough to keep most of us from taking late evening walks along the Amazon River.

The smallest snake is found on the Caribbean islands of Martinique, Barbados, and St. Lucia. It is a thread snake that is only about 4½ inches (11.5 centimeters) long.

BIRDS

The ostrich of North Africa is the biggest. Males average 8 feet (245 centimeters) in height and 275 pounds (125 kilograms) in weight. One fellow tipped the scales at 345 pounds (156 kilograms). No wonder they can't fly!

The smallest bird is the bee hummingbird, found in Cuba and on the Isle of Pines. The males have body lengths of about 2½ inches (6.5 centimeters). They weigh a fraction of an ounce (about 2 grams).

AMPHIBIANS

The Chinese giant salamander is the biggest. One huge individual measured about 5 feet (150 centimeters) from the tip of its snout to the end of its tail. It weighed almost 100 pounds (45 kilograms).

The smallest amphibian is an arrow-poison frog of Cuba, which is less than ½ inch (1.25 centimeters) long.

FISH

The whale shark is the largest, and it lives in the warmer parts of the Atlantic, Pacific, and Indian oceans. One whale shark was 59 feet (18 meters) long and weighed 90,000 pounds (41,000 kilograms). However, these creatures won't star in a remake of *Jaws*—they feed on tiny ocean plants and animals, **not on people.**

The smallest fish is the dwarf pygmy goby, found in freshwater streams and lakes in the Philippines. It is about ¼ inch (.5 centimeters) long—the smallest animal with a backbone.

SKATEBOARDING: SURFING ON WHEELS

In the early 1960's some California teen-agers attached roller skates to wood boards so they could practice "surfing" on the sidewalk. This skateboarding fad was short-lived because bumpy roads and stones stopped the small skate wheels and sent the sidewalk surfers sprawling. That wasn't much fun, so the skaters went back to surfing in the sea.

A few years later, however, someone made bigger and wider wheels out of polyurethane plastic. These were softer than the roller-skate wheels, and they rolled over stones and bumps and gave excellent traction. These wheels were mounted to special shock absorbers, called trucks, which made the boards easier to maneuver. The boards, too, were improved.

With the new equipment, skateboarding really caught on, and the number of skateboarders grew every year. Today, more than 20,000,000 people are regular riders—in the United States, Canada, Japan, Venezuela, France, Switzerland, Brazil, and many other countries.

▶ COMPETITIVE SKATEBOARDING

Skateboarding has come a long way since the 1960's. In addition to the millions who are skateboarding just for fun, there are people who are skating to win. Today skateboarding is a competitive sport—for both professionals and amateurs.

Professional skateboarders compete, both individually and in teams, for big prize money. They also give demonstrations, endorse products, and appear in television commercials. Most of these athletes are in their teens or twenties, but the skateboarding star of one Pepsi commercial was only five years old.

A few of these athletes are making very good livings as professional skateboarders. Eighteen-year-old Ty Page, an outstanding skateboarder with the nickname "Incredible," was expected to make nearly $100,000 in 1977 by winning contests and endorsing skateboard equipment. And 16-year-old Laura Thornhill expected to earn $60,000 in a year as a pro skateboarder.

These pro skateboarders are competing in the men's slalom.

Not all competitive skateboarders are pros. Some are keeping their amateur status so they can compete in the Olympics—if skateboarding is accepted as an Olympic event. These youngsters can join any of the amateur teams that are forming and competing with each other.

▶ THE BIG CONTESTS

Competitive skateboarders can enter several championship categories, including downhill speed racing, slalom, cross-country, and freestyle.

The men usually prefer downhill racing, competing against each other or against the clock. They also like slalom—weaving at breakneck speeds around plastic cones, just as slalom skiers do around poles.

The women seem to enjoy freestyle most. To music, each competitor performs her own ballet on a skateboard. She designs the routine to show her skill and skateboarding style. Her routine often includes high jumps; handstands; and 360's—which means turning around in circles on one pair of wheels, similar to an ice skater pirouetting on skates.

Safety equipment is very important in competitive skateboarding. The athletes always wear helmets, elbow pads, knee pads, socks and shoes, gloves, and sometimes wrist bracers. If a skateboarder falls, the safety equipment will prevent serious injury. One skateboarder was especially thankful he was wearing padded leather gloves when he lost his balance during a pro competition. His hands hit the pavement at over 50 miles per hour (80 kilometers per hour), but he walked away from the spill unhurt. Some downhill speed racers are now wearing all-leather suits during competition, which make them look more like motorcycle racers than skateboarders.

▶ SKATEBOARD PARKS

It is often difficult to find a large, smooth, and safe area in which to skateboard. For this reason, special skateboard parks are being opened everywhere. In California alone, more than 25 outdoor skateboard parks were under construction in 1977. And in some places, these special parks are being built indoors so that people can skateboard in the winter months.

A young skateboarder takes her turn in the women's freestyle high jump.

These parks have concrete hills, bowls, and flat areas where skateboarders can practice wheelies, 360's, kick turns, tail slides, handstands, and other maneuvers. Some parks even have long courses for cross-country practice.

After learning how to keep their balance and make some easy maneuvers, skateboarders like to zoom around the concrete bowls. The higher you climb toward the upper edge, the more you seem to defy gravity. (During some championship competitions, teammates encourage each other to "hit the lip"—ride as close as possible to the top of the bowl without shooting over its edge.)

Skateboard parks are great places to have lots of fun. They are also excellent places to practice if you want to become a professional or amateur competitor.

▶SKATEBOARD MODELS

There are many different skateboard models. You have a choice of wood (oak, ash, teak, mahogany, or layers of maple veneer), as well as plastic, fiberglass, or aluminum. Prices range from $10 to $110. Or you can buy blank boards, trucks, and wheels separately, and assemble your own custom model.

Some skateboards have been adapted for other kinds of enjoyment. One model is fitted with handlebars so it can be used as a scooter. On another model, you can attach a mast and sails to the board, using wind power to skate. You can even buy a motorized skateboard.

▶SAFE SKATEBOARDING

Follow these rules for safe skateboarding:

• Always wear shoes when skateboarding; athletic shoes are best because they give you a good grip on the board.

• Wear a helmet, gloves, knee pads, and elbow pads, even for skateboarding around the neighborhood.

• If you fall a lot and usually land on your hands, wear wrist guards. If you keep landing on your hips, wear hip pads. Or wear skateboarding pants with padding sewn in the seat.

Safety equipment is very important for skateboarders. This youngster wears a helmet, elbow and knee pads, shoes and socks, and gloves.

• Take good care of your equipment and inspect it before you ride. Check the board for cracks or splits and make sure all nuts and bolts are tightened. Be certain that the trucks are adjusted properly and that wheels and bearings are turning freely.

• Try to skate in areas designated for skateboarding, such as skateboard parks.

• If you are allowed to skateboard on the sidewalk, watch out for pedestrians.

• When skateboarding in the street, obey traffic signals and signs, and all traffic regulations.

• Never skateboard in a busy street, or in a street where it is difficult for motorists to see you.

• Never allow a bicycle, car, or other moving vehicle to tow you while you are on a skateboard.

• Always be courteous to other skateboarders and people you meet while skateboarding.

• Set a good example so you do not give skateboarding a bad name.

▶ FOR MORE INFORMATION

There are three magazines devoted to the sport of skateboarding: *Skateboard World, Skateboarder,* and *Wide World of Skateboarding.* The magazines feature interviews with the pros, discuss the latest equipment, describe the newest skateboard parks, and announce upcoming contests.

The International Skateboard Association is trying to promote safe skateboarding throughout the world, and to establish skateboarding as an accepted recreational and competitive sport. If you would like to learn more about pro and amateur skateboarding, as well as how to go about setting up a skateboard park where you live, write to the International Skateboard Association, 711 W. 17th Street, Costa Mesa, California 92627.

If you live in Canada, you can write to the Canadian Skateboard Association, 102 Bloor Street West, Toronto, M5S 1M8.

MICHELE AND TOM GRIMM
Authors, *Hitchhiker's Handbook*

Anne Bonny and Mary Read became very good friends.

LADIES ON THE HIGH SEAS

Today we believe that women can do whatever men can do, and go wherever men can go. But not too long ago, women were regarded as the "tender sex." They were thought to be dainty, delicate, and sensitive. Imagine how shocked people were when they heard that there were lady pirates. And that these "ladies" could be as cruel and bloodthirsty as the men!

In the early 1700's, one of the most famous of these women pirates was Anne Bonny. Anne had been born in Ireland. When she was very young, she and her parents moved to the Carolinas. Her father, a wealthy and respected planter, looked forward to the time when his daughter would make a "proper" marriage. But Anne was a rebellious teenager.

In time, Anne met a young sailor and married him—without her father's approval. Her father was so angry, he made her leave home. Anne and her husband went to New Providence, an island in the Bahamas where many sailors and pirates gathered. There, Anne's husband deserted her. But Anne did not remain alone for long. She met and fell in love with Calico Jack, a famous pirate. This handsome daredevil and his crew regularly attacked ships in the Atlantic Ocean and Caribbean Sea. Anne was completely fascinated by the stories of his adventures. When Calico Jack was ready to return to sea, he asked Anne to go with him, and she quickly agreed.

Anne soon became very handy with her pistols and cutlass. She stood at Calico Jack's side as they boarded and plundered ship after ship. On one of the ships they captured was what appeared to be a young man. This person either volunteered or was forced to join Calico Jack's crew, and quickly became a tough and ruthless pirate. Imagine everyone's surprise when this person turned out to be a young woman—Mary Read!

Mary had been brought up in England. She had worked on a ship and had even fought in the army—always disguised as a man. When Anne Bonny discovered that the fierce pirate fighting alongside her was a woman, the two became very good friends.

Their happy but evil life on the high seas was soon to end, however. In October, 1720, the pirates were anchored off the coast of Jamaica. Suddenly a British ship appeared. Calico Jack and the other male pirates hid belowdecks, refusing Mary's demands that they come up and fight the attacking sailors. Mary and Anne bravely tried to fend off the sailors, but they were finally overpowered. All the pirates were captured, and Calico Jack, Anne,

Mrs. Ching was a brave fighter.

and Mary were convicted of piracy. As Calico Jack was led to his execution, he saw Anne for one last time. She offered little sympathy, saying she was "sorry to see him there, but if he had fought like a man, he need not have been hanged like a dog."

Anne and Mary were imprisoned. Mary caught a terrible fever and died in prison. Anne remained in prison and eventually gave birth to a child. But to this day, no one knows what finally happened to her.

▶ **ONE HUNDRED YEARS LATER . . .**

A much more important lady pirate lived in China, almost 100 years later. Her name was Ching Yih Saou. Mrs. Ching's husband had been a pirate in command of a fleet of 600 ships. When he was killed, his wife took over the fleet. Soon it had 800 large ships and almost 1,000 smaller ones.

Mrs. Ching was a well-organized, efficient businesswoman. She was also a smart leader and a brave fighter. Her fleet of ships was divided into six squadrons. Each was led by a lieutenant. Like Calico Jack, they had colorful names: Jewel of the Whole Crew, Frogs' Meal, Scourge of the Eastern Sea.

The pirates were allowed to have their wives on board. When the pirates attacked other ships or sailed up rivers to loot and burn villages, the women fought right alongside their husbands.

The Chinese emperor tried to end the pirates' reign of terror. In 1808 there was a big battle between Mrs. Ching's ships and a fleet of government ships. Mrs. Ching won. The government sent out a second fleet. It was quickly captured by the pirates. A third fleet was sent out. This time many of Mrs. Ching's ships were destroyed and many pirates were killed. But Mrs. Ching survived and soon was back in business. The government made a few more attempts to stop her, but none were successful.

Then the emperor tried a different approach. He offered to pardon the pirates if they would stop their terrible activities. One of Mrs. Ching's lieutenants—together with his 8,000 men and 160 ships—accepted. Mrs. Ching was angry. But when she thought more about it, the pardon seemed like a good idea, and she and her crew accepted the emperor's offer.

So Mrs. Ching stopped terrorizing the seas. But she never became a law-abiding citizen. Instead, she spent the rest of her life as the head of a big smuggling operation.

Anne Bonny, Mary Read, and Ching Yih Saou were the best-known women pirates—there were probably others. They chose and were successful in a "profession" that was believed to be for men only. And, although their acts were crimes, they achieved a certain kind of equality by being what they were—ladies on the high seas.

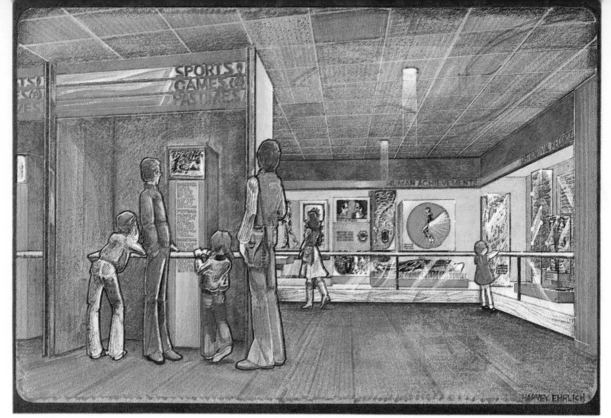

The Guinness World Records Exhibit Hall in New York City.

IT'S A WORLD RECORD!

How long was the longest beard ever grown? What is the largest seed? How much did the heaviest person of all time weigh?

In 1976 the Guinness World Records Exhibit Hall opened in New York City. And there you can see displays on all of these: the 17½-foot (5.3-meter) beard, the double coconut, the man who weighed 1,069 pounds (485 kilograms).

But you don't even have to leave your home to learn what's biggest, fastest, longest, deepest, brightest, or earliest. Just pick up the *Guinness Book of World Records*. It will tell you that Kelly Stanley of Canada needed only 36 seconds to climb a tree 90 feet (27.5 meters) tall. That Martin Luther King, Jr., was the youngest person (35) to receive the Nobel Peace Prize. That the longest telephone call was made by college students in Michigan—it lasted 1,000 hours.

This fascinating book was the idea of an executive of Guinness, a brewing company in Ireland. He thought it would be a nice gift for the company's customers. Two young men, Norris and Ross McWhirter, were hired to gather facts and write the book. The first edition

came out in 1955. A new edition, with new records, is published every year. About 30,000,000 copies of the *Guinness Book of World Records* have been printed—and you can buy the book in 17 languages.

There are about 20,000 records, and countless facts about them, in the *Guinness Book*. Many can be used to stump your friends: What is the longest bone in your body? (the thighbone). Which planet has the most moons? (Jupiter, with 14). What boxer scored the most knockouts in his career? (Archie Moore, who had 141).

Some of the records are almost unbelievable. But no matter how strange they seem, they are true. Two men dropped fresh eggs from a helicopter 600 feet (183 meters) above the ground—and the eggs didn't break. A young Australian ate 63 bananas in 10 minutes. A U.S. park ranger has been hit by lightning 6 times—and has lived to tell about it.

Even you can be in the book. To become eligible, you must break a record or do something interesting that no one else has done. In 1977, for example, Samson Kimombwa ran the 10,000-meter race (10,936 yards) in 27 minutes and 30.5 seconds—setting a new world record.

Can you better that?

AMAZING RECORDS SET BY YOUNG PEOPLE

1887 15-year-old Charlotte Dod wins the women's championship at Wimbledon, the youngest person ever to win at this famous tennis tournament.

1913 11-year-old Henry Chambers is named organist at Leeds Cathedral in England, the youngest person ever to be appointed organist of a church.

1938 10-year-old Shirley Temple's wealth as a movie actress totals over $1,000,000; she is the youngest woman ever to earn that much money.

1944 15-year-old Joe Nuxhall begins pitching for the Cincinnati Reds, the youngest person ever to become a major league baseball player.

1962 4-year-old Dorothy Straight writes *How the World Began.* It's published two years later, making her the youngest person ever to have a book commercially published.

1965 12-year-old Karen Muir sets a new world record in the women's 110-yard backstroke (about 100 meters), becoming the youngest person ever to hold a major world sports record.

1970 17-year-old Sally Younger is clocked at 105.15 miles per hour (169 kilometers per hour) on water skis, the fastest any woman has ever gone on water skis.

1975 14-year-old Jim Sparks sits in a tree for more than 61 days, the longest anyone has ever sat in a tree.

1976 13-year-old Robert Knecht does 7,026 push-ups in 3 hours and 56 minutes, the most push-ups ever done at one time.

1977 19-year-old Cindy Nicholas swims nonstop across the English Channel and back in 19 hours and 55 minutes, setting a new world record. And she is the first woman ever to do it.

PUT-OUT PUP

"You naughty pup," scolded Nanny, wagging her finger at Lucky. "Digging under the fence was bad enough. Now you're stealing cookies."

Lucky caught sight of the pile of cookie crumbs nearby. "Not again!" he thought. It was the second time that week he'd gotten in trouble for something he hadn't done. He wished his mother and father hadn't left him in charge when they had gone on a holiday with Roger and Anita, their humans.

First Nanny had seen him filling in the hole that Rolly had dug under the fence and had mistakenly blamed him. And now these incriminating cookie crumbs! It was probably Rolly again. He was always hungry.

Nanny carried Lucky to the corner and plopped him down. "Now you stay there until you've mended your ways," she ordered.

While Lucky was sitting in the corner, he happened to notice a trail of crumbs leading to a hole in the base of the wall.

Lucky peered in and there sat the biggest, fattest mouse he'd ever seen, licking cookie crumbs from the corner of his mouth.

"You took those cookies," growled Lucky. The mouse looked up, not a bit surprised to see the pup.

"Of course it was me. I'm a mouse," he said. "My compliments to Nanny. She's an excellent cook." The brash mouse began licking the last cookie crumbs from his whiskers.

"Delicious," he added. "My family and I are definitely moving in. They'll be here tomorrow and it looks as though we'll be neighbors. My name is Rayford T. Mouse, Esquire, but you may call me Squire."

"I won't call you anything," said Lucky angrily. "You won't be here long enough. Not when my brothers and sisters and I get through with you. We don't allow mice in this house."

Squire Mouse sat back on his haunches and laughed. "You foolish pup! I suppose you think a bunch of wet-nosed puppies are going to run me out. Well, I've been around a long time, and I don't leave a house until I'm good and ready. Besides, this house suits me perfectly. It has a well-stocked pantry. It's warm and cozy. Nanny makes cookies on Thursdays. And above all else, it doesn't have any cats."

With that, the mouse scampered out of the hole, flicking Lucky in the nose with his tail as he

headed back to the kitchen for a second helping of Nanny's cookies. Lucky was furious. He ran after the mouse, but old Squire proved too fast and he led Lucky on a merry chase around the room. So intent was Lucky on catching the mouse that he didn't see the reading lamp in his path. Lucky barreled right into the stand, and over it went with a crash.

Nanny flew into the room. "Oh, you bad puppy!" she gasped when she saw Lucky sitting amid the remains of the shattered lamp.

"I don't know what's gotten into you this week," she said, shaking her head. "Maybe a little time outside will discourage your talent for mischief." She dropped the pup gently on the back porch and closed the door.

Lucky was feeling very sorry for himself. He didn't like being on the wrong side of Nanny—particularly when he hadn't done anything to deserve it.

"Hello, pup," said a voice from atop the backyard fence.

Lucky looked up to find Tom, the neighborhood alley cat, sunning himself.

He didn't like Tom, whose habit it was to sit on the fence and tease the puppies whenever he wasn't busy digging in ashcans.

"Did dear old Nanny put you out?" asked the cat in a jeering tone. "What seems to be the problem?"

Normally Lucky would have answered with a growl, but he was feeling very sorry for himself and needed a sympathetic ear. He told Tom all about the mouse.

"Old Squire moved in, eh? You've really got problems now. You should see the size of his family. Of course, I could help you out . . ." offered the cat as he lazily arched his back and yawned.

"You could?" asked Lucky, who suddenly saw a solution to the mouse problem.

"Sure," said Tom. "For a price."

"What kind of a price?" asked Lucky suspiciously.

"I've been waiting for a chance to put Nanny on my feeding route, but I can't get close to her with all you pups underfoot. You let me win Nanny over and I'll take care of your mouse."

The prospect of having the cat around permanently didn't appeal to Lucky, but under the circumstances he agreed to the terms.

He instructed Tom to come back late that night through a broken window in the basement.

"I'll see that the basement door to the kitchen is left open a crack," added Lucky.

That night after dinner Lucky held a family conference with his brothers and sisters. He told them all about the mouse trouble and the bargain he had made with the cat.

"Oh, pooh!" said Rolly. "We could catch that mouse ourselves."

"Maybe yes and maybe no," Lucky cautioned. "His family moves in tomorrow and we don't have time for a mistake. He's got to go tonight and I think Tom is the one to make sure that he does."

All the puppies agreed.

Late that night Tom slipped into the house, where he found Lucky anxiously awaiting his arrival.

But to Lucky's surprise, the cat headed straight for the kitchen table, jumped up and started making a meal out of Nanny's cream pitcher.

"You're supposed to be catching the mouse," snapped Lucky.

"Plenty of time for that," muttered the cat between slurps of cream.

Lucky realized he'd been tricked by the cat and ran to wake his brothers and sisters. When he returned, there were fourteen angry puppies on his heels and they began yipping and growling.

"You pups keep quiet," hissed the cat as he made his way toward the butter dish. He was just

about to make a meal of it when the kitchen light snapped on. There stood Nanny in the doorway with a broom in her hand.

"Yikes," screeched the cat, and he jumped off the table, sending the butter dish crashing to the floor. Tom made a dash for the basement door, but the puppies headed him off.

Down came Nanny's broom, just missing Tom's hindquarters. The frightened cat took off like a shot into the dining room.

Around and around the room they went. Tom was yowling and screeching as Nanny's broom crashed down behind him again and again. The puppies were barking and yipping as they nipped at the cat's heels.

Tom was very relieved when Nanny finally caught up with him and tossed him out the front door.

"That's enough excitement for tonight, puppies," Nanny announced after she closed the front door. "Back to bed." And she dutifully tucked each puppy back into the warm, cozy box.

Lucky waited until he was sure Nanny was back upstairs before he crept out of the box and padded softly over to the mouse hole.

"I guess I'll just stand guard here all night and do the best I can to discourage the mouse invasion," thought Lucky.

He hadn't been there long when old Squire Mouse poked his head out of the hole. "Out of my way," he commanded as he scurried past Lucky with a suitcase under each arm.

"I'm leaving! Couldn't get a wink of sleep in this house with all the confounded noise going on. I'm trying the house next door. It's a bit drafty, and there are no cookies on Thursdays. But there are no cats. And above all, there are no noisy puppies!"

Lucky smiled as he watched Squire Mouse disappear down the basement stairs.

THE NUTCRACKER

It's Christmas Eve. A little girl named Mary is having a wonderful time at her family's party. She and her friends are playing games and dancing. Soon the presents are given out. Mary's godfather gives Mary a wooden Nutcracker doll dressed in a uniform of red and blue. Mary loves her Nutcracker doll, even though it isn't very handsome.

After the party is over, the family goes to sleep, but Mary leaves her bed and goes back to the living room, where she has left her Nutcracker. Cradling it in her arms, she falls asleep on the sofa.

Suddenly, noises awaken her. She opens her eyes and sees that the Christmas tree is growing taller and taller. Her toys are growing too, and soon they are as big as she is. A group of giant mice rush into the room, scaring Mary.

The Nutcracker has also grown. He and the toy soldiers have come to life, and they battle the mice with swords and a cannon. Just as the Mouse King tries to attack Mary, the Nutcracker kills him. The other mice run away.

The living room fades away. Mary finds herself in a beautiful forest. Coming toward her is the Nutcracker, who has changed into a handsome Prince. Hand in hand, they walk off into the distance.

As morning comes, Mary and the Prince reach the Land of Sweets—a wonderful place where the streets are made of candies and the buildings are of fancy cakes and cookies. Traveling in a ship made of gilded walnut shells, the young travelers sail down rivers of lemonade and orange juice to the palace of the Sugar Plum Fairy.

The fairy invites the children to sit on a throne made of white icing. They are given cakes and ice cream and many other delicious things to eat. And they are entertained by dancing food from all over the world: chocolates from Spain, teas from China, coffee from Arabia. Even the Sugar Plum Fairy and her handsome Cavalier dance for them.

But it's time to leave. Mary and her Prince fly off in a sleigh pulled by reindeer. As they leave, the Sugar Plum Fairy and all the other wonderful people in the Land of Sweets wave good-bye.

And so ends *The Nutcracker,* one of the world's favorite stories. Each year, hundreds of dance groups perform this fairy-tale ballet. Sometimes the story is slightly different. For example, in some versions the little girl's name is Clara. She wakes up at the end, as if the whole adventure had just been a dream.

Many of the parts in *The Nutcracker* are danced by young people, including the party guests, the soldiers, the mice, and, of course, Mary and the Prince.

The Nutcracker is an enchanting experience—for the children on stage as well as those in the audience. It's just what each of us wishes would happen on Christmas Eve—or any other night of the year.

Mary loves her wooden Nutcracker doll, which she received as a Christmas gift.

The Nutcracker and the toy soldiers have come to life and battle the mice.

Dancing foods from all over the world perform in the Land of Sweets.

1. Crayons are made of wax and colored powders called pigments.

2. The liquid wax and the pigment of one color are mixed together in a huge vat.

3. After wax and pigment are blended, the liquid is poured into crayon molds.

4. After wax has hardened, the crayons are removed from the molds and inspected.

5. The crayons are labeled, and then an assortment of colors is put into boxes.

6. After lids are put on, these boxes of crayons are ready to be shipped.

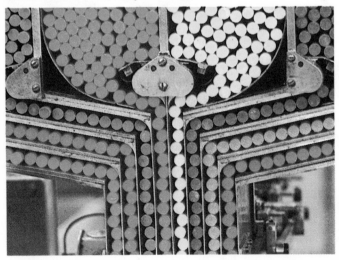

RAINBOW IN A BOX

Name any color you can think of and it is probably in a box of crayons. Red, yellow, purple, black, green, blue, white. Then there are some surprising colors, too, ones you never even thought of. Apricot, thistle, mulberry, and salmon might also be found in a crayon box. Some boxes have as many as 72 different shades of crayons. And they're all there waiting to be used in your coloring book, on your party decorations, or for a special school assignment.

Did you ever wonder when crayons were invented? Or how they are made? Crayons certainly aren't something new. As far back as the Stone Age, people were using a kind of coloring stick to decorate the walls of their caves. They often drew pictures of the wild animals that roamed the land. It must have taken a lot of color sticks to draw a huge mammoth.

Thousands of years later, artists drew pictures with colored sticks of chalk. These sticks were called crayons and they are the ancestors of our modern crayons. The wax crayons that we use today were first invented about 100 years ago. At that time they came in just one color—black. It was not until 1903 that the first assortment of 16 colors was produced. Since that time more and more colors have been added to the selection, and today the crayon box is a rainbow of colors.

Let's take a tour through one of the most colorful places in the world—a crayon factory. Here we can see how today's crayons are made. It's a fairly easy process, but a lot of care has to be taken so that the color and texture of each one is perfect. Crayons have to be soft enough to leave a mark when you draw a picture or make a decoration, but at the same time sturdy and long-lasting.

Just follow the numbers and you'll see how a "rainbow in a box" is made.

PREDICTING EARTHQUAKES

It was a lovely, quiet morning in Southern California's San Fernando Valley. A bright, sunny day was predicted. The date: February 9, 1971. The time: 6 A.M.

Seconds later, powerful shock waves tossed people out of bed, toppled buildings, and knocked down concrete highway bridges. It was an earthquake—the area's worst since 1933. The tremor lasted less than a minute, but it killed 64 people and injured 1,000 others.

Every year earthquakes kill people and destroy their homes. They cause billions of dollars worth of damage. There is no known way to stop earthquakes. But scientists are learning how to predict them. If people could be told when and where an earthquake will occur, they could leave the area before the quake hits. Ambulances, fire trucks, helicopters, and other emergency forces could be ready to rush to the quake area.

It is even possible that scientists will be able to predict quakes several years in advance. This would enable a community to check buildings to make sure that they are sound. Buildings not strong enough to withstand a quake could be fixed or torn down.

In recent years scientists have correctly predicted more than twenty quakes. The first quake to be correctly predicted in the United States was a small one in the Adirondack Mountains of New York. The second was a slightly bigger quake in California.

Let's look at the clues scientists are studying in their efforts to predict earthquakes.

▶ CAN ANIMALS WARN OF EARTHQUAKES?

In ancient times the Chinese believed that animals acted strangely before an earthquake. Chinese scientists still believe this—and they are slowly convincing other people that animals make excellent earthquake predictors.

At Stanford University in California, some people were studying chimpanzees. On two occasions they noticed that the chimps were very, very restless. Both times the animals' unusual activity occurred just one day before a quake.

A scientist studying cockroaches found that these little insects also became exceptionally active right before a quake. And Japanese scientists have evidence that fish move into different waters a day or two before a quake.

No one knows why animals act strangely before a quake. And this behavior would be of value only if it occurred long enough before the quake for people to take action. Once, hundreds of rats started running through the streets of Cape Town, South Africa. (What a frightening sight that must have been!) A few minutes later an earthquake hit the city. The few minutes warning given by the rats was not enough time for people to flee the quake.

In early 1975 many animals in northeastern China began behaving very oddly. Pigs bit one another. Cows fought. Turtles cried. Snakes stopped hibernating and came out of their winter dens. Chickens flew to the tops of trees. Prompted largely by this unusual animal behavior, scientists warned people in the area that an earthquake would occur. Buildings were evacuated. People left cities for the countryside. On February 4 a very strong quake struck, within a few hours of the predicted time. Damage was severe, but Chinese officials believe that many thousands of lives were saved by the warning.

▶ PRESSURE WAVES

Just as unusual animal behavior seems to signal a coming earthquake, an unusual pressure wave pattern on a seismograph is now believed to be a warning signal too. (A seismograph is an instrument that measures the pressure waves in the earth's crust.) Scientists have recently noticed that seismographs sometimes record a sudden slowing of the speed of pressure waves passing through certain underground rocks. The pressure waves then return to their normal speed. And shortly after their return to normal, an earthquake occurs.

Here is what scientists believe this unusual pattern on the seismograph is recording. Rocks under pressure are laced with many tiny cracks. These cracks are filled with underground water. Pressure waves travel through these water-filled cracks at a certain regular rate of speed.

If stress on the rocks increases greatly, the cracks inside the rocks suddenly spread and widen. Because the cracks have grown larger so suddenly, they are no longer completely filled with water. Pressure waves always travel

Can strange animal behavior be an earthquake warning signal? This is what happened prior to an earthquake in China: pigs bit one another, cows fought, turtles cried, and chickens flew into trees.

more slowly through dry space than through water-filled space; so the seismograph is recording that the pressure waves have slowed down. But later, when underground water seeps in and completely fills up the enlarged cracks, the pressure waves return to normal. And very soon after this, the rocks, which have been terribly weakened by the wide cracking and the increased water pressure, break apart in an earthquake.

Something else that happens when the rocks in the earth's crust come under tremendously increased stress is a swelling, or bulging, of the earth's surface. Along the San Andreas Fault in California, the earth has bulged as much as 10 inches (25 centimeters). Sometimes such

bulging has been followed by a quake. There was, for example, such a bulge in the San Fernando Valley shortly before the 1971 quake.

Not all earthquakes have been preceded by bulges. And sometimes bulges have formed but no big earthquake has followed. Still, scientists want to know what's happening underneath any bulges.

In the past decade, scientists have learned a great deal more about earthquakes. Many of them believe that accurate earthquake prediction will soon be a reality. Once scientists reach this goal, they will turn their attention to learning to prevent and control earthquakes.

JENNY TESAR
Consultant, Curriculum Concepts, Inc.

59

THE SMITHSONIAN'S INSECT ZOO

On a sidewalk near the Smithsonian Institution in Washington, D.C., a honeybee finds treasure—melting ice cream dropped by a careless child. Follow that bee! It will lead you to a fascinating place—the Insect Zoo.

This new zoo is actually a very large room in the Smithsonian's National Museum of Natural History. And the honeybee lives there. The bee has its own special entrance to the building, and to its hive. You must use another entrance to go in. But once you're in the zoo, you can wander over and look inside the four-level hive where the honeybee and all its relatives live. And there are lots of other things to see too.

There are more than 1,000,000 kinds of insects in the world. They vary greatly in shape, color, size, life-style, and movement. They make different sounds and eat in different ways. At the Insect Zoo you will see thousands of insects, various types leading their lives in various ways. You may see a large rhinoceros beetle feeding on a banana; a tomato hornworm eating a tomato plant; a lubber grasshopper chewing on a head of lettuce; an ant falling into a pit that was dug by a doodlebug; water beetles swimming in a pond; the hatching of a beautiful butterfly.

The zoo also has some relatives of insects, such as spiders, centipedes, and millipedes. One of the most popular attractions is the tarantula—especially at dinnertime. Its dinner is a cricket, and you can watch the tarantula capture and eat it. Because tarantulas may eat only once a week, the zoo has seven of them. A different tarantula is on display—and being fed—each day of the week.

Another interesting exhibit in the zoo shows insects that sometimes live in people's homes and gardens. There are termites, eating wood that could be part of a house. There are cockroaches under a sink. And there are Colorado potato beetles, causing the same kind of damage as they do in a farmer's field.

Insects and their relatives have been around for over 400,000,000 years. They live in every part of the world. At the Insect Zoo you will learn many fascinating things about these tiny neighbors of yours.

Would you like to hold the hickory horned devil? (This insect larva will eventually become a moth.)

The honeybees have their own special passageway between their hive and the outside world.

The male scarab beetle fascinates these youngsters.

A LITTLE FAIRY CASTLE

It's the most magnificent of castles. There are dishes made of solid gold. The chandeliers sparkle with diamonds and other precious gems. There is silver furniture, and on the walls are paintings of Snow White, Alice in Wonderland, and Old King Cole.

Does this sound like a fairy tale? Well, in a way it is. The castle is real—but it is in miniature. It measures 9 by 9 feet (3 by 3 meters), and its highest tower reaches 12 feet (3.5 meters) in height. And all the wonderful things in it are tiny—so tiny, you can hold them in your hand.

The little castle is in Chicago's Museum of Science and Industry. It was given to the museum by actress Colleen Moore as a gift to the children of the world. The castle was built on a dream, a dream we've all had—to live in a fairyland, with all the wonderful characters from the stories we have read.

So pretend you are a tiny prince or princess, only 5 inches (13 centimeters) tall. Here is your castle. Come along and take a walk through fairyland.

Step into the great entrance hall. Go over to the silver table where your gold crown is. The princess's crown is covered with pearls and has a green emerald in the center. The prince's crown and scepter are set with rubies and sapphires.

In this great hall are some of the many tiny treasures you have collected on your travels. There are the chairs of the Three Bears, the harp that Jack stole from the giant who lived atop the beanstalk, and Cinderella's glass slippers.

▶ CINDERELLA AND KING ARTHUR

Relax for a few minutes in the drawing room. Its walls are covered with paintings that tell the story of Cinderella. From the ceiling hangs a chandelier gleaming with diamonds, emeralds, and pearls. Its electric light bulbs, each the size of a grain of wheat, light up the room. The floor is of rose quartz and green jade, and was made in China.

Sit on a silver chair. Or perhaps you would like to play the piano. The little pieces of paper you see are sheet music—all handwritten by the composers themselves. George Gershwin

A little fairy castle.

gave you a copy of *Rhapsody in Blue.* Irving Berlin gave you "Alexander's Ragtime Band." Richard Rodgers gave you "Oh! What a Beautiful Morning."

Time passes quickly. Soon the "Hickory Dickory" grandfather clock tells you that it is time for dinner. As you walk into the dining hall, be careful not to break the amber vases, one on either side of the doorway. They are more than 500 years old, and actually belonged to the Dowager Empress of China.

This room looks like King Arthur's dining hall. The marble walls are covered with needlepoint tapestries that tell of the deeds of King Arthur. You sit down at the Round Table and begin eating your meal, which is served on gold plates.

Next door, in the kitchen, cooks are preparing your dessert. Water for your hot chocolate is in a kettle on a copper stove that looks just like the stove in which the wicked witch wanted to lock Hansel and Gretel!

▶ OLD FATHER NEPTUNE AND ALI BABA

You tell the butler that you'll have dessert in the library. This room reminds you of the great voyages you have made across the oceans to find your treasures. The copper and bronze fireplace looks like a fishnet—and holds Old Father Neptune and two mermaids in its folds. Over the fireplace is Captain Kidd, guarding his pirate chests. Over one doorway is a sculpture showing Robinson Crusoe and his man Friday. Over the other is Gulliver capturing the fleet of the Lilliputians' enemies.

Now comes the best part—your most unusual library of books. Sir Arthur Conan Doyle, F. Scott Fitzgerald, Booth Tarkington, Edna Ferber, and other well-known authors have given you special editions of their writ-

The Cinderella drawing room.

King Arthur's dining hall.

The bedroom of a prince.

ings. And every book is just the right size for your tiny hands.

Here is your book of autographs, filled with the signatures of famous people: Winston Churchill, Henry Ford, Dwight D. Eisenhower, Queen Elizabeth II, Admiral Byrd.

Is that the sound of horses? Look out the window. There's Cinderella's silver coach. It has stopped for a minute so the horses can drink from the copper fountain.

Let's go up to the treasure room. The only way to get into it is through an ironbound trapdoor. Speak the secret words, and Ali Baba, who guards the riches, will let you enter. In this room are magic rings, decanters filled with love potions, and all your souvenirs of fairyland parties.

Before you go to sleep—for even fairy princes and princesses must sleep—we'll quietly step into the chapel for a moment. Look at the lovely stained-glass window, which depicts stories from the Bible. Touch the gold and ivory organ. Here is a Bible from 1840, the smallest in the world. It is bound in gold and red leather, and contains the entire New Testament.

And now to sleep.

▶ BEDROOMS FIT FOR A KING OR A QUEEN

Here in the prince's stately bedroom is a wondrous collection of swords, including King Arthur's magical Excalibur. Two gold cannons are on a chest, and in a corner is a pair of red seven-league boots — exactly what every prince needs for his travels around the world. The carvings on the bed and chairs depict a Russian fairy tale.

As you enter the princess's room, you will notice that over the door is Peter Pan—dancing on a mushroom. The princess's room is very feminine. The walls are white, decorated with gold, and the floor is made of mother-of-pearl. A pair of diamond and emerald chairs sparkle with beauty. On the ivory dresser is a tiny gold set of comb, brush, mirror, and nail file. The canopied bed is also made of gold, and is shaped like a boat. It is the bed on which Sleeping Beauty slept for 100 years—until she was awakened by the prince.

As you lie in bed, your thoughts of the day fade into dreams. You dream that you have suddenly grown very big—as big as a human being. That might be fun—almost as much fun as being a fairy prince or princess who lives in this wonderful fairy castle.

THE FLIGHT OF THE LONE EAGLE

Thousands of people were massed around Le Bourget airfield just outside Paris, France, on the night of May 21, 1927. They waited anxiously, all eyes focused on the dark sky overhead. Somewhere in that vast black sea of space, a lone American flier was winging his way toward Paris in a fragile, single-engined monoplane.

The man at the controls was Charles A. Lindbergh, Jr., a boyish-faced, 25-year-old former mail pilot and stunt flier. And the big question was, would he make it? Would he successfully complete his transatlantic flight from New York to Paris?

The thousands gathered at Le Bourget believed that "Lucky Lindy," as the newspapers called him, could do it. Hours went by. The night grew cold. Still they waited.

Suddenly the sound of an engine was heard. Giant searchlights lit the sky. There was a loud cheer as the crowd caught sight of a silver-gray plane. Moments later, at 10:24 P.M., Charles Lindbergh brought his plane, the *Spirit of St.* *Louis*, safely down to earth. The crowd went wild. A tidal wave of people broke through a cordon of police and soldiers and rushed madly toward the plane.

Cheering Frenchmen shouting "*Lindbergh! Vive Lindbergh!*" pulled the tall, slender American out of the cockpit and hoisted him onto their shoulders. Pale and weary, the youthful aviator managed a smile as he said simply: "Well, I made it."

Indeed he had. On that memorable night in 1927 Charles Lindbergh became the first person to complete a solo nonstop flight across the Atlantic. Nicknamed the "Lone Eagle," he became an instant world hero and a legendary figure in his own lifetime.

In 1977 the United States and France celebrated the 50th anniversary of Lindbergh's incredible feat of courage and flying skill. Special events were held. Commemorative stamps were issued. And on May 20, 1977, an exact copy of the *Spirit of St. Louis* took off from a Long Island, New York, airport in a re-enactment of

"All the News That's Fit to Print."

The New York Times.

THE WEATHER
Generally fair today and tomorrow; moderate to fresh southerly winds.

Section 1

VOL. LXXVI...No. 25,320. NEW YORK, SUNDAY, MAY 22, 1927. FIVE CENTS

LINDBERGH DOES IT! TO PARIS IN 33½ HOURS;
FLIES 1,000 MILES THROUGH SNOW AND SLEET;
CHEERING FRENCH CARRY HIM OFF FIELD

COULD HAVE GONE 500 MILES FARTHER

Gasoline for at Least That Much More— Flew at Times From 10 Feet to 10,000 Feet Above Water.

ATE ONLY ONE AND A HALF OF HIS FIVE SANDWICHES

Fell Asleep at Times but Quickly Awoke—Glimpses of His Adventure in Brief Interview at the Embassy.

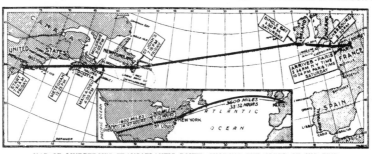

MAP OF LINDBERGH'S TRANSATLANTIC ROUTE, SHOWING THE SPEED OF HIS TRIP.

CROWD ROARS THUNDEROUS WELCOME

Breaks Through Lines of Soldiers and Police and Surging to Plane Lifts Weary Flier from His Cockpit

AVIATORS SAVE HIM FROM FRENZIED MOB OF 100,000

Paris Boulevards Ring With Celebration After Day and Night Watch—American Flag Is Called For and Wildly Acclaimed.

CAPTAIN CHARLES A. LINDBERGH,
Who Flew Alone Across the Atlantic, New York to Paris, in Thirty-three and One-half Hours.

the historic flight. (The original *Spirit of St. Louis* is on display at the Smithsonian Institution in Washington, D.C.)

▶ FIFTY YEARS EARLIER

The event these activities commemorate began on the morning of May 20, 1927, when Charles Lindbergh climbed into his silver airplane and prepared to take off from Roosevelt Field on Long Island.

Lindbergh was one of many aviators who were competing for a $25,000 prize that was being offered to the flier, or fliers, who could make a nonstop trip across the Atlantic from New York to "the shores of France."

From the moment he learned of the contest, Lindbergh decided to accept the challenge. At 25, the lanky Midwesterner (called "Slim" by his friends) was already an experienced pilot. All he needed was a good plane. And thanks to a group of St. Louis businessmen, Lindbergh got the money he needed to have one built according to his own design. He named it the *Spirit of St. Louis* in honor of his backers.

Lindbergh had two main rivals for the $25,000 prize: Commander Richard E. Byrd and Clarence Chamberlain. Both these men had copilots. Lindy was the only one who would fly alone.

Rain and fog kept the competitors grounded for days. But on the morning of May 20, Lindbergh decided to chance it. With his plane loaded down with 451 gallons (1,707 liters) of fuel, he taxied onto the runway. It was a tense moment. The rain had left the field a soggy mass of mud and it wouldn't be easy to get up enough speed to lift the overweighted plane off the ground. But Lindbergh was a determined man. He pulled back the stick and felt the aircraft quiver.

Several times the plane lurched off the ground, only to drop down again. Finally, the *Spirit of St. Louis* soared into the sky—barely missing a tangled web of telephone wires at the end of the runway. The time was 7:52 A.M. The Lone Eagle was airborne.

Lindbergh had no radio on board and his only navigating instruments were a compass and a chart on which he had carefully plotted his route. Because of the way the plane was constructed—with the engine and fuel tanks in front of the cockpit—Lindbergh could not see directly ahead. He had to poke his head out of the side window or use a small periscope he had brought along.

Eleven hours after leaving Roosevelt Field, Lindbergh flew past the rocky eastern coast of Newfoundland and out over the open sea. Now he was completely on his own. He still had most of his 3,600-mile (5,800-kilometer) flight ahead of him and he would have to fly through thick fog and storm clouds much of the way. There was also the problem of staying awake during the long flight.

The plane itself helped him to stay alert. It was not a stable aircraft, and if he loosened his grip on the controls, it would drift off course, jolting him back to his senses. Other times he would stick his head out of the cockpit and let the wind and rain revive him.

Much of the time, Lindbergh flew close to the water, sometimes only 20 feet (6 meters) above the waves. His big fear was that he would run smack into an iceberg or the masts of an oncoming ship.

Occasionally, he climbed as high as 10,000 feet (3,000 meters) to avoid a storm. Once during the night hours, he flew so high that ice began to form on his wings. But Lindy spotted it before it could cause the plane to stall, and he dropped down to where the air was warmer.

By the 24th hour, Lindbergh was in a half-awake, half-asleep state. His body was numb from fatigue, his joints ached. But as darkness gave way to light on the morning of May 21, he got his second wind. In the afternoon his spirits rose when he spotted a fishing boat. Lindy brought his plane down and buzzed the little vessel. A man stared up at him from one of the portholes, and the aviator shouted: "Which way is Ireland?" The startled boatman was too stunned to answer, and Lindbergh could only hope that he was headed in the right direction. He was. Soon after this encounter, he spotted a coastline. Ireland!

At about 8 P.M. he passed over Cornwall, England. An hour later he was over the coast of France. He had done it. At that point he could have landed and claimed his prize, for the rules were that the pilot had only to reach the "shores of France." But Lindy wanted to go the whole route—to Paris. And so he continued on, landing at Le Bourget airfield shortly after 10 P.M. (Paris time). He had completed his New York to Paris flight in 33½ hours.

For Charles Lindbergh the long ordeal was over and a lifetime of fame was about to begin. Decorated by the governments of France, Britain, and Belgium, "Lucky Lindy" returned in triumph to the United States. Several million New Yorkers turned out for the traditional tickertape parade up Broadway. In Washington, D.C., President Calvin Coolidge awarded him the Distinguished Flying Cross. Until his death in 1974, Lindbergh remained the idol of millions.

▶**FIFTY YEARS LATER**

Today the new Concorde supersonic jet can make the trip from Paris to New York in just 3½ hours—one tenth the time it took Lindbergh. But not even the Concorde's record-breaking flying time can dim the luster of "Lucky Lindy." Charles Lindbergh made his transatlantic flight alone, in a small, single-engined plane, without computers and modern instruments to guide him. His courage and endurance will never be forgotten.

HENRY I. KURTZ
Author, *Captain John Smith*

YOGURT—A NATURAL FOOD

The exact origin of yogurt is not known. But we do know that this important dairy product dates back to biblical times—and beyond. Yogurt was probably first eaten in the Middle East. In that region's hot climate, milk spoils rapidly. For this reason yogurt, which does not spoil easily, was a welcome discovery. Yogurt no doubt developed sometime in the distant past when certain bacteria accidentally got into some stored milk.

That is what yogurt is today—milk in which two friendly strains of bacteria have been grown. The names of these micro-organisms are *Lactobacillus bulgaricus* and *Streptococcus thermophilus.*

How is yogurt made? In its most common form, yogurt is made from cow's milk. Much of the fat is often removed and nonfat milk solids with extra protein are added. The milk is homogenized, pasteurized, and then injected with the bacteria. Sometimes fruit preserves and other ingredients are added. But in natural yogurts, no artificial flavor, color, or preservatives should be used.

The milk, now containing the bacteria, is piped into machines that fill the yogurt cups you see in the stores. These cups are then stored in incubators until the product reaches a custard-like thickness. Throughout this process, temperatures must be carefully controlled for the yogurt to develop properly.

Yogurt is a food with many uses. It is a good source of protein, calcium, certain B vitamins, and minerals. Because of its nutritional value, many people eat yogurt as a supplement to their regular diet or as a snack between meals. It can be enjoyed by itself or combined with other foods, such as peanut butter or dry cereal. Many cooks use yogurt in recipes for salad dressings, party dips, desserts, and main dishes.

Yogurt is a popular food in many parts of the world. In Finland it is called *glumse,* in Norway *kyael meelk,* and in Russia *prostokvasha.* In India, the Balkans, and the Middle East, yogurt is used in many dishes.

Food markets in the United States offer different types of yogurt. There is the sundae-style yogurt, with fruit on the bottom; Swiss-style, with fruit throughout; and western-style, with fruit on the bottom and fruit coloring and sweetening on top. Two of the most popular types of yogurt are frozen yogurt on a stick and soft-frozen yogurt served in cups or cones from machines.

Some people make yogurt at home with their own yogurt machine. The instructions, which come with the machine, must be followed carefully. For example, unless the milk is kept at the right temperature, the bacteria cannot live. The result would then be sour milk, not yogurt.

JUAN E. METZGER
Chairman, Dannon Milk Products

Making yogurt at home—so easy that two children can do it.

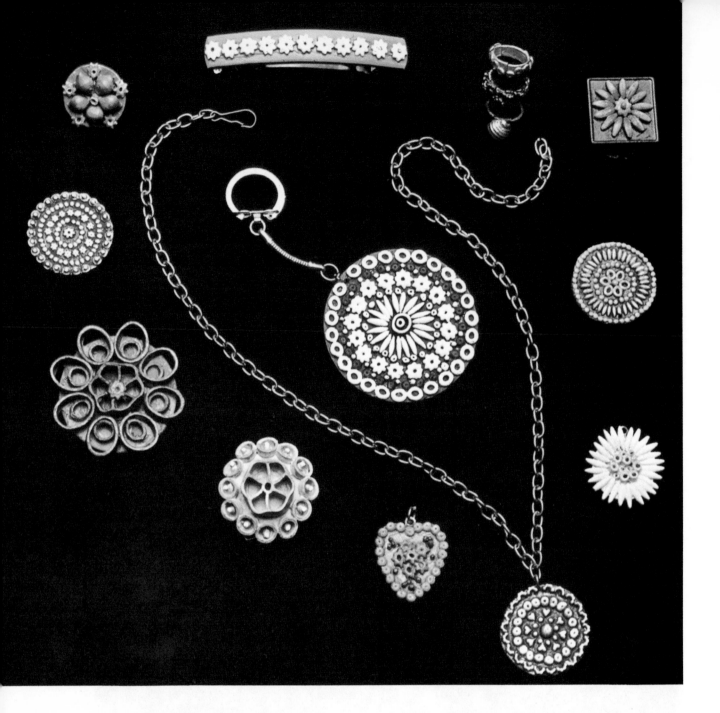

PASTE AND PASTA

It's fun. It's easy. It's inexpensive. In just a short time and with a handful of pasta, you can make toys, jewelry, and many other things. The craft is called macaroni magic . . . or noodle doodle . . . or paste and pasta.

All you have to do is take a plain object, decorate it with different kinds of pasta, and then cover it with bright paint. In this way you can change a plain piece of wood into a sign saying "My Room." A heart-shaped piece of cardboard becomes a brooch. A tin can turns into a vase or a pencil holder. A wooden building block becomes a paperweight.

Here's what you need:

• Items to decorate. These can include things made of wood, metal, plastic, stone, or glass.

• Pasta. There are almost 1,000 different shapes of pasta from which to choose. Select stars, wheels, elbows, shells, circles, squares, alphabets, or long straight spaghetti. Start with what you can find in your kitchen.

• Glue. White craft glue is good for wood, cardboard, and stone. Use model-airplane glue on glass, metal, and plastic.

• Acrylic paints.

• Acrylic spray. This seals the surface and makes the object easy to clean.

Let's turn a flat piece of wood into a paperweight. **Here's what to do:**

1) Be sure the wood is heavy enough to hold down a pile of papers and is clean.

2) Arrange pasta on the wood in any design that pleases your eye.

3) Glue the pasta—one piece at a time—onto the wood. When you have finished gluing on all the pieces, let the object stand until the glue is dry.

4) Paint the entire object. You may want to use two or more colors. For example, you could paint the entire object, including the pasta, pale green. After the first coat dries, paint the tops of the pasta dark green. (Or you may want to paint just the pasta and leave the wood natural.)

5) When you have finished painting and the paint is dry, cover your paperweight with a coat of clear acrylic spray.

There's almost no end to the items you can decorate. And even if you can't find anything to decorate, you can make something just with pasta. A necklace, for instance, by stringing together painted elbow macaroni. Or snowflakes for the Christmas tree by gluing together pasta circles of different sizes. Or a toy car from lasagna and manicotti noodles.

So get your paste and pasta, and begin!

DJIBOUTI

The Republic of Djibouti is one of Africa's newest nations. Formerly known as the French Territory of the Afars and the Issas, it became independent in 1977. Djibouti is a small, sparsely populated desert land with virtually no natural resources. Its chief assets are its strategic location at the southern entrance to the Red Sea, its port and capital, also called Djibouti, a railroad, and French military bases.

▶ THE PEOPLE

Estimates of the population of Djibouti vary considerably, since many of its people are nomads. Their existence in an inhospitable land depends on constant traveling in search of

The Great Mosque in the city of Djibouti. Almost all the people of the country are Muslims.

pasture for their herds of camels and flocks of goats and sheep. Often the herdsmen cross into neighboring countries seeking new pasture. It has been said that there are about twice as many goats in Djibouti as people, who number approximately 125,000. About half the population lives in the city of Djibouti.

The two main ethnic groups are the Afars, who have close ties to neighboring Ethiopia, and the Issas, who are related to the people of nearby Somalia. There are also some Europeans, chiefly French, and Arabs in the coastal towns. Except for the Europeans, almost all the people are Muslims. Languages spoken include French, Afar, Somali (spoken by the Issas), and Arabic. The coming of independence has little affected the nomadic people of the interior, who still live much as their ancestors did.

▶ THE LAND

Djibouti has an area of 8,800 square miles (23,000 square kilometers). It is located in northeastern Africa, just north of the landmass known as the Great Horn. It is bordered by Ethiopia on the north, west, and south, by Somalia on the southeast, and by the Gulf of Aden on the east.

Most of the country consists of arid plains, but there are mountains that rise to a height of 5,000 feet (1,500 meters). A narrow coastal plain lies along the Gulf of Aden. The land is barren and desolate with sharp cliffs and deep ravines. About 90 percent of the country is classified as desert. Most of the rest is pastureland. The vegetation is made up largely of thorn shrub, cactus, and sparse grasses, which provide meager grazing for the herds and flocks of the nomads. There are a few irrigated orchards and palm groves. Overgrazing of the land has led to soil erosion throughout most of the country.

▶ THE CLIMATE

The climate is very hot. From May to October temperatures average 92° F (33° C), and temperatures as high as 113° F (45° C) have been recorded. The weather is only slightly cooler between November and April. Through part of the year, winds blowing from the Arabian desert across the Gulf of Aden bring dry air and no moisture. Rainfall is scanty.

THE ECONOMY

Djibouti has no useful mineral deposits or other natural resources except for livestock. About half the population lives by animal herding. There is some fishing, and a few people make their living from the soil. With practically no arable land, almost all the country's food must be imported. There is almost no manufacturing except for soft drink bottling companies and meat processing plants.

The mainstay of the economy is the port of Djibouti, which lies in a natural harbor on the Gulf of Tadjoura, an inlet of the Gulf of Aden. It is a free port, which means that no customs duties need be paid. Djibouti owes much of its importance to its location on the waters leading to and from the Suez Canal, and the city is a port of call for ships using the canal. Many of the people in the city work on the docks and in ship repair shops.

A second important source of income is the railroad, which links Ethiopia with the port of Djibouti. The port is Ethiopia's main outlet to the sea and is thus vital to that country's economy. Over 50 percent of Ethiopia's imports and exports pass through Djibouti by way of the railroad.

The French military garrison, which remained in Djibouti after independence, also provides some revenue. In addition, France contributes an annual subsidy to keep the economy going.

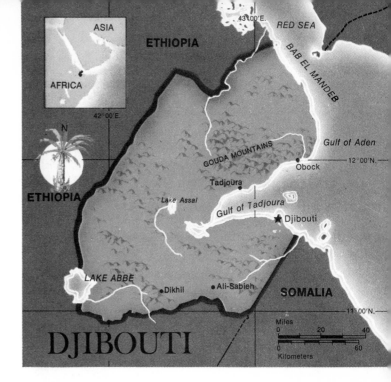

DJIBOUTI

FACTS AND FIGURES

REPUBLIC OF DJIBOUTI is the official name of the country.

CAPITAL: Djibouti.

LOCATION: Northeastern Africa. **Latitude**—10° 52' N to 12° 43' N. **Longitude**—41° 48' E to 43° 25' E.

AREA: 8,800 sq mi (23,000 km²).

POPULATION: 125,000 (estimate).

LANGUAGE: French, Afar, Somali, Arabic.

GOVERNMENT: Republic. **Head of state**—president. **Head of government**—prime minister. **International cooperation**—Arab League.

ECONOMY: Agricultural products—livestock, dates, garden vegetables. **Industries and products**—transit trade, ship's supplies, hides, soft drink bottling, meat processing. **Chief exports**—hides, cattle, coffee (in transit from Ethiopia). **Chief imports**—food, cotton goods, cement, chemicals. **Monetary unit**—Djibouti franc.

HISTORY AND GOVERNMENT

Because of its nearness to the Asian continent, Djibouti was long an arrival point for migrations from Asia to Africa. Between the 8th and 10th centuries Arabs converted the people of the region to Islam. The French became interested in the area in the 19th century and signed treaties with the local chiefs. The French wanted influence in the region to counter British influence in Aden—now Yemen (Aden)—across the Red Sea. After the Suez Canal was opened and Britain became active in Egypt, France claimed a protectorate over the area—in 1885. The colony was known as French Somaliland. It remained a protectorate until 1958, when it became a French overseas territory.

The name French Territory of the Afars and the Issas was adopted in 1967 after the people voted to keep their country an overseas territory of France. Ten years later, however, the people voted for independence, which was declared on June 27, 1977.

The two problems facing Djibouti are the lack of a true economic base upon which to develop the country, and the claims of its larger neighbors, Ethiopia and Somalia. Ethiopia regards the railroad link with Djibouti as vital to its interests. Somalia has traditionally claimed the land in which the Issa people live. Djibouti's future depends on whether these problems can be solved.

HUGH C. BROOKS
St. John's University

73

A silver jubilee portrait of Queen Elizabeth.

THE QUEEN'S JUBILEE

For our Monarch and her people,
United yet and free,
Let the bells ring from every steeple
Ring out the Jubilee.

From "Jubilee Hymn" by Britain's
Poet Laureate, Sir John Betjeman

Once upon a time there was a lovely princess who lived in a faraway land across the sea. She was no fairy-tale princess, however. She was the real heir to an ancient throne. Her name was Elizabeth and her father was King George VI, ruler of the British Empire.

One day the 25-year-old Princess Elizabeth and her husband, Prince Philip, were deep in the jungle of Kenya, at the start of a trip to Britain's colonies and possessions. On that morning of February 6, 1952, word reached Elizabeth that her father, the king, had died.

She was no longer a princess—she was the queen. A little over a year later, in June, 1953, the shy, solemn young woman was formally crowned Queen Elizabeth II in a magnificent ceremony that thrilled the world.

In 1977, Queen Elizabeth and her subjects celebrated her silver jubilee—the 25th anniversary of her becoming queen.

And what a celebration it was. The year-long festivities included pomp and pageantry throughout Britain and in the many Commonwealth countries that the queen visited.

The celebration that was held in Britain was truly spectacular. British people from all walks of life joined together in a great outburst of patriotic feeling and warm affection for the woman who had been their queen for a quarter of a century.

The jubilee was officially opened on May 4, 1977, when the queen addressed both houses of Parliament in London's historic Westminster Hall. But the main festivities took place a month later.

On the night of June 6, Queen Elizabeth lit a bonfire on a hill near Windsor Castle. Within a short time, 100 other fires were lit, forming a chain from the northernmost reaches of Scotland to the Channel Islands off England's southern coast. The signal fires brought to mind the beacons that had warned the British of the approach of the Spanish Armada in 1588, during the reign of Queen Elizabeth I.

The lighting of the bonfires touched off a week of festivities that included pageants and parades, village fairs, and fireworks displays. The highlight of the Silver Jubilee was a royal procession to St. Paul's Cathedral in London, where a special thanksgiving service was held.

It was a Cinderella-like spectacle. The queen rode from Buckingham Palace to St. Paul's in

the gold State Coach, which was drawn by eight gray horses. Prince Philip, wearing his medal-bedecked admiral's uniform, was at her side. Plumed cavalrymen, looking like knights of old, and a troop of Royal Canadian Mounted Police escorted the queen's coach. More than a million people lined the streets to cheer their queen.

State trumpeters sounded a fanfare as the queen entered St. Paul's to be greeted by colorfully dressed government officials, many in traditional wigs and long gowns. There were also dignitaries from all over the world.

During the service, the Archbishop of Canterbury praised the queen, citing her life as "an example of service untiringly done, of duty faithfully fulfilled, and of a home life stable and wonderfully happy."

Still more pageantry followed the next day as the queen and other members of the royal family sailed up the Thames River. They were saluted by hundreds of ships and boats of every description. And that night a brilliant display of fireworks lit up the sky over the Houses of Parliament.

In the words of one British newspaper, the jubilee week was "a jolly good party." It was also a time for the British people to reaffirm their faith in the nation's constitutional monarchy, in which the sovereign "reigns but does not rule." (The real power of government is in the hands of a prime minister and the cabinet.)

Not all Britons cheer the queen, however. Some feel that the monarchy is outdated, a relic of the past. But the overwhelming majority of the British people (nearly 90 percent according to recent polls) believe that the queen serves an important function.

The monarch is the symbol of national unity, say her supporters, and a rallying point in time of trouble. Today, when the once vast British Empire has shrunk to a few tiny possessions, the queen is a reminder of a glorious past. She provides a comforting sense of continuity in a world of rapid change.

As one British statesman put it, "The Americans have their Constitution and their flag. In addition to our flag, we have our queen."

HENRY I. KURTZ
Author, *Captain John Smith*

ARTISTS OF THE CANADIAN ARCTIC

The Canadian Arctic is a cold, barren land. Vast fields of snow and ice are broken by glacier-covered mountains. In the dead of winter the sun never shines. At the height of summer it shines 24 hours a day—yet the ground remains permanently frozen.

But there is life here. Billions of birds make their nests in this land. Caribou herds move across the plains. Seals and walruses swim in the waters. And there are human beings—the Eskimos, descended from people who first came to the Canadian Arctic some 5,000 years ago.

They came from Asia, across the Bering Strait. These early people were nomadic—they didn't live in towns but wandered from place to place. They were hunters who followed the caribou herds, searched for the birds' nesting grounds, and caught fish and seals and walruses. They were people who used every part of whatever they took from their environment. For example, a walrus provided them with food (its meat); clothing (its skin); and tools for sewing and cutting (made from its bones).

During the endless winter nights, when a family rarely left its house of snow, the people carved bones into useful items. Perhaps a small mask or a tiny figure of an animal or person would be fashioned from the bone. These sculptures probably had religious value or were used in the practice of magic.

It wasn't until the 19th century that the Eskimos came into regular contact with white men. Most of the white men who traveled into the Canadian Arctic were traders. They wanted furs. Sometimes an Eskimo would carve something to sell or give to the traders. However, rarely was anything intentionally carved as "art."

But life was changing. White people moved farther north, building towns and bringing industry where caribou once roamed. White hunters killed huge numbers of caribou. The Eskimos found the wandering existence more and more difficult, because there wasn't enough game to feed all the people.

By the late 1940's it became obvious that new ways of survival had to be found. It was then that the economic value of Eskimo art was realized and that people were encouraged to create sculpture and other artifacts that could be sold in the outside world.

Today, art—especially carving, but also printmaking—is a major source of income for some Eskimos. The sculptures are carved primarily in whalebone, walrus ivory, and stone. They usually depict three major subjects.

Animals and the hunt. Eskimo artists often carve powerful polar bears, sleek seals, swimming sea birds, and watchful caribou. They make carvings of the men who spend long hours trying to catch the animals: a hunter standing over a hole in the ice, waiting for a seal to come up for a breath of air; a man lying in wait on the frozen ground, his harpoon close at hand; a fisherman carrying his catch of fish; a man with a dead fox slung over his shoulders.

Family and community. The family is very important to Eskimos, and one of the most common subjects of their art is a mother and her child. A sculpture might show the mother holding a child in her arms. Or the child might be nestled on the mother's back, in a special pouch in her parka hood.

Fantasy. Many carvings depict spirits, myths, and legends of the Eskimo people. There are carvings of sea goddesses and the merman, bear spirits and sea spirits, priests and sorcerers. Sometimes a sculpture shows an Eskimo with a spirit. For example, there is one in which an Eskimo is removing lice from the spirit's fur.

Almost all Eskimo art shows traditional scenes and beliefs. But life in the Canadian Arctic has changed in recent years. Dogsleds are giving way to snowmobiles. Snow houses and tents of animal skins have been replaced by prefabricated plywood homes. Instead of caribou meat, people eat canned foods.

There are other influences of the white people, especially on the children, who go to English-speaking schools. There are comic strips and radios and airplanes. The children learn about Santa Claus and television and lands where it is always warm.

Will today's young artists of the Arctic continue to depict the same subjects that were important to their parents and grandparents? Or will their art reflect the mixed white and Eskimo world they are now growing up in?

An Eskimo family after the hunt.

Eskimos playing a stick game.

An Eskimo hunter.

SPORTS BRIEFS

Batter up! Sculptor Claes Oldenburg's "Batcolumn" is a new addition to Chicago's impressive skyline. Many people think that "Batcolumn" is an unusual work of art. But Oldenburg feels that the latticed steel sculpture, which is 100 feet (30 meters) high, symbolizes nothing more than what it is —a baseball bat. The sculptor (*on the right*) has dedicated it as "a monument both to baseball and the construction industry."

Muhammad Ali retained his world heavyweight boxing title in a championship match on September 29, 1977, at Madison Square Garden. The judges awarded Ali a unanimous decision over his opponent, Earnie Shavers, in a tough fight that went the full 15 rounds.

The America's Cup, awarded by the New York Yacht Club, is the most sought after international sailing trophy. The famous race, which takes place every three years, was held again in 1977. The U.S. entry *Courageous* was the defending champion, and it beat the yacht *Australia* in a four-race sweep in the best-of-seven series.

Twenty-eight-year-old Toller Cranston starred in one of Broadway's biggest hits in 1977. But it was not a drama, a comedy, or a musical. It was his "The Ice Show," a blend of figure skating, dancing, and theater. The enthusiastic audiences were thrilled by his unique style. Born in Ontario, a province in Canada, Cranston began skating at an early age. He has won many figure-skating championships, and placed third at the 1976 Winter Olympics.

A TOUCH OF BEAUTY

Heavy snowfalls can be cruel acts of nature. They often cause great hardships for people and severe damage to property. But some people welcome snowstorms because of the beauty they bring to the cold, barren winter landscape.

What do you feel when you see snowflakes falling? Perhaps you think about building snowmen, sledding with friends, skiing, and snowball fights. Or perhaps you think about how lovely and fragile the snowflakes are.

But did you ever wonder where those snowflakes come from? Or what they are made of?

A snowflake is actually a clump of ice crystals. Each crystal is a tiny six-sided figure. A snowflake begins its life in a cloud, as a microscopic speck of matter such as a grain of dust or a tiny splinter of another ice crystal. Molecules of water freeze onto this speck, and the crystal grows and grows until it finally falls to earth as a snowflake.

Perhaps you've heard that no two snowflakes are the same. It's true—but you'd have to look at the flakes through a microscope to see this for yourself. The snowflakes you see here have been greatly enlarged so that you can enjoy the beauty of their designs.

HODGEPODGE

Keys. Hats. Bottle caps. Picture postcards. Sugar cubes in different wrappings. Tree roots. Put these all together and what do you have? A hodgepodge.

That was the name of a very popular exhibition at the children's museum in Karlsruhe, a city in West Germany. Hodgepodge—What Children Collect was planned and put together entirely by children. They did all the work. They even wrote texts describing their exhibits and telling why they collect the things they do.

There were 19 collections in the exhibition. They were put together by children between the ages of 4 and 14 who like to collect things.

One 4-year-old girl makes dolls from seashells. An 8-year-old boy makes pictures from bird feathers he finds on the ground. One young boy collects hats: army caps, hats from flea markets, and hats from his grandfather. Another child collects all sorts of keys.

There are many ordinary things that can be collected. Matchbooks are an example. There are many different designs on them. Corks from wine bottles are also fun. Many have words or even designs stamped on them.

Do you collect anything? If you don't, why not start? The children in Karlsruhe are sure you will find that it's a lot of fun.

LEAPIN' LIZARDS! IT'S LITTLE ORPHAN ANNIE

Move over, Charlie Brown, Dennis the Menace, and Blondie. Look who has stepped out of the comic pages and landed on Broadway as the biggest hit of the 1976–77 theater season. It's Little Orphan Annie; her faithful dog, Sandy; and Daddy Warbucks. They're all part of a big smash musical called *Annie*.

Annie isn't an overnight sensation who came upon fame and fortune in the theater. Little Orphan Annie had a long history before she hit Broadway. For more than 50 years Annie, Sandy, and Daddy Warbucks had one adventure after another in the comic pages of daily newspapers. Annie—with her mop of curly hair, red and white dress, and huge blank saucer-shaped eyes—captured the hearts of millions of readers. Her favorite expressions, "Gloryosky!" and "Leapin' Lizards," became household words.

Now don't run off to get a newspaper to look for Annie. She's no longer there. The comic strip ended several years ago. But don't despair—Annie and her friends have come to life on the Broadway stage.

The Broadway *Annie* is not really the same as the newspaper Annie. The show uses the same characters that appeared in the comic strip, but a new story line has been added. As the curtain rises, Annie and her six little orphan friends are living in the New York Municipal Orphanage. The year is 1933 and America is in the middle of a terrible depression. Nearly everyone is poor and jobless.

But no one is unhappier than these orphans. They are watched over by the strict and wickedly funny Miss Hannigan, keeper of the orphanage. She gets angry at any sound of happiness coming from the children, and at four o'clock in the morning orders the poor little girls to scrub the floor to a high shine. And as if that isn't enough, gruff Miss Hannigan threatens to stamp out their freckles!

Ah . . . but wait. Something wonderful is about to happen. Oliver Warbucks, one of the richest men in the world, decides to invite an orphan to spend the Christmas holidays with him. Annie is the lucky one who is chosen. And the rest is pure happiness, much to Miss Hannigan's dismay. During the visit Annie charms Oliver Warbucks, and he decides to adopt her.

There are many wonderful songs and dances along the way, and of course there are some evil people who try to put a stop to the good times. But as the curtain comes down, Annie and Daddy Warbucks—and Sandy—are living happily in the Warbucks mansion.

▶ GLORYOSKY! IT'S ANDREA McARDLE

What would *Annie* be without the kids? An unthinkable situation. After all, the seven young orphans are probably the most important part of the story. The girls range in age from 7 through 14, and they are loaded with talent. In their orphanage dresses, they sing and dance their way into the hearts of the audience. But one orphan stands out. She's the one who leaves Miss Hannigan behind and steps into the wonderful world of Daddy Warbucks. She's Annie, the star of the show.

And just who is playing rags-to-riches Annie, the best Broadway role in years? Why, none other than 13-year-old Andrea McArdle of Philadelphia, Pennsylvania. Andrea has been performing since she was three years old, mostly in TV commercials and regional theaters. She also played the role of Wendy on the television soap opera "Search for Tomorrow," for which she won the 1976 award as best juvenile actress on afternoon TV.

Andrea came to the part of Annie quite by accident. She was originally cast as one of the other orphans. While the show was playing a pre-Broadway run in Connecticut, the young actress who had been playing Annie left the cast. Andrea learned the role in two days and went on to play Annie in Washington, D.C., and finally New York.

It's not easy being a leading lady, however. Living the life of a Broadway star doesn't excuse Andrea from her schoolwork. Tutors meet with Andrea and the other young members of the cast every day to go over lessons and homework assignments. The only "young person" in the cast to be excused from schoolwork is Sandy, Annie's lovable dog.

It seems that Andrea has adjusted to her new life and is settling in for a long Broadway run. She's even had her dressing room at the theater wallpapered with Little Orphan Annie cartoons!

Stepping out of the comic pages and landing on Broadway: Daddy Warbucks, Little Orphan Annie, and Sandy.

The orphans—minus Annie—sing their way into the hearts of the audience.

Rich John, Poor John

"TWENTY BAGS OF MY GOLD!" Evil Prince John bellowed at the Sheriff of Nottingham. "Do you mean to tell me that Robin Hood took twenty bags of my gold from the Royal Tax Collector's coach and you did nothing to stop him?!" Prince John was so mad, his ears were turning purple!

"Please, Sire," the Sheriff replied, "I can't be everywhere at once! I was guarding the Royal Mint!"

"What idiot told you to guard the Royal Mint?"

The Sheriff cleared his throat. "You did, Sire."

Prince John decided it was time to change the subject. "It's bad enough that outlaw steals my gold, but then he gives it away to the poor!" The greedy monarch shuddered at the thought of anyone giving away gold—especially *his* gold!

"That's what I get for being rich," John groaned. "If I were poor, Robin Hood would be *giving* me gold, instead of taking it away from me."

Suddenly Prince John's face brightened. "Sheriff," he beamed, "I think I've thought of a way to get my gold back!"

"You mean . . . " began the Sheriff.

"Precisely!" John chortled. "Now here's what I want you to do . . . "

Early the next morning the Sheriff of Nottingham jumped on his horse and galloped from one end of the kingdom to the other, spreading the news that Prince John had squandered his last gold piece. The Prince was now poorer than the poorest man in the kingdom! At first nobody believed it.

"Very well," said the Sheriff. "If you don't believe me, why don't you go up to the Castle and see for yourself."

The citizens of Nottingham looked at each other and said, "That's not a bad idea." So off they went, up the hill and over the drawbridge, until they were standing in front of Prince John's castle. The first thing they saw was the "For Sale" sign nailed to the front door. They went closer to the Castle and peeked in all the downstairs windows.

"All the soldiers are gone!" said the first citizen of Nottingham.

"All the servants are gone!" said the second citizen.

"All the furniture in the castle is gone!" said the third citizen.

"And Prince John's gone, too!" said the fourth citizen.

"The Sheriff is telling the truth! Prince John *is* broke! Just wait until Robin Hood hears about this!"

And all the citizens ran back over the drawbridge and down the hill. They kept running until they got to Sherwood Forest and Robin's camp.

Robin Hood, however, was out of town at an archery contest, and had left Little John in charge of his Merry Men. So the citizens broke the news of Prince John's newly found poverty to Robin's second-in-command.

When the Merry Men heard the news, there was great rejoicing. Then Little John held up his hand for silence. "Hold on, boys. Robin's principle has always been, 'steal from the rich and give to the poor.' If Prince John is poor now, we'll have to give him back his gold."

A stunned silence fell over the merrymakers.

Allan-a-Dale was the first to speak. "Isn't that carrying principles a bit too far, Little John?"

"A principle is a principle," that ever-honest outlaw replied. "We took the gold from rich Prince John—we must give it back to poor Prince John!"

In vain the Merry Men argued that it wasn't Prince John's gold in the first place. But it was no use. Little John had made up his mind. "Load the bags of gold on the hay wagon," he ordered.

Half an hour later, the wagon was rolling down the road to Nottingham. "How are we going to

find Prince John?'' asked Allan. ''He doesn't live at the castle anymore.''

''I've already thought of that,'' replied Little John. He took an envelope from his pocket. It was addressed to Prince John. ''We'll send this letter to him and follow the mailman!''

When they got to town they dropped the letter off at the Nottingham Post Office. When the mailman came out to deliver it, they just followed him. The mailman went directly to the poorest section of town and deposited the letter in a very poor-looking mailbox that stood in front of a very poor-looking house.

Little John and Allan-a-Dale got down off the wagon and knocked on the door of the shabby, unpainted house. Prince John opened the door. He looked very poor, too.

''Here are the twenty bags of gold we took from your Royal Tax Collector yesterday when you were rich,'' said Little John.

''Oh, bless you, kind sir!'' Prince John replied gleefully.

The two outlaws unloaded the gold in front of Prince John's ramshackle shack. ''We'll be back tomorrow with the fourteen bags of gold I took from your Royal Mint last week,'' said Little John, turning the horse and wagon toward Sherwood Forest once again.

Then, as the wagon disappeared down the street, Prince John called into the house. ''Okay, you guys, all clear! Come on out and help me get this gold into the house.''

The Sheriff and Sir Hiss emerged from the house, and the three of them carried the heavy bags of gold inside.

At once, Prince John sat down on the floor and began to untie one of the bags.

''What are you doing, Sire?'' Sir Hiss hissed.

''I'm going to count it!'' John answered.

''You mean you don't trust Robin Hood?'' the Sheriff said.

''I don't trust anybody,'' answered the Prince. ''It's a principle of mine. Now help me get these bags open.''

Meanwhile, Little John and Allan-a-Dale were bumping down the road toward home. ''I don't trust that guy,'' Allan said.

''Well, what can we do?'' Little John answered. ''A principle is . . . ''

Allan finished the sentence. ''A principle. Yeah, I know.''

Suddenly Little John said, ''What's that funny noise in the back of the wagon?''

''I didn't hear anything,'' said Allan.

Little John pulled up the horses and stopped the wagon. ''There's something rattling around back there!''

Both men went to the back of the wagon. There, on the floor of the cart, were two gold pieces!

"They must have fallen out of one of the bags of gold we gave to Prince John," Allan said.

"Well, there's only one thing to do," said Little John, climbing back into the driver's seat. "We'll have to go back and give them to Prince John. Robin would never approve of cheating the poor!"

Inside the Prince's shack the three rascals were so busy counting that they didn't hear the wagon stop outside. As the two honest outlaws reached the door, they heard loud laughter. "That's the Sheriff's voice," said Little John.

"And I hear Sir Hiss in there, too!" added Allan.

They crept silently around to the back of the shack and listened at the window.

"It's the best scheme you ever had, Your Majesty," they heard Sir Hiss say. "As long as Robin Hood thinks you're poor, he'll have to keep giving you gold."

"Keep quiet and count," Prince John ordered gruffly.

Outside, beneath the window, Allan and Little John looked at each other. "We've been hoodwinked!" whispered Allan.

Little John nodded. "What do we do now?"

Allan reached into his pocket and drew out the two gold pieces they had found in the wagon. Stealthily, he reached through the window and slipped a gold coin under the Sheriff's belt. Then he slipped the other coin under Sir Hiss's belt. Then he dropped back down under the window again.

Suddenly they heard Prince John exclaim, "There are only 998 pieces of gold here! Two pieces of gold are missing! Where are they?"

Little John and Allan-a-Dale carefully rose to look into the room. Prince John had jumped to his feet.

"Robin Hood must have cheated you, after all!" said the Sheriff, starting to stand up, too. As he did, a gold coin fell from beneath his belt. It hit the floor with a loud clink. The Sheriff stared at the coin, amazed.

"I think *you* tried to cheat me!" Prince John said angrily.

"But, Sire . . . " the Sheriff stammered. "I didn't . . . "

Sir Hiss uncoiled. "I told you not to trust the Sheriff," he started to say. Another gold piece hit the floor.

"Aha!" boomed Prince John. "I'll teach you two to try and cheat me!"

Sir Hiss and the Sheriff came to the quick conclusion that Prince John was in no mood to listen to explanations. Both ran for the door, Prince John hot on their heels.

When they were gone, Little John and Allan-a-Dale scooped up all the gold and put it in their wagon. As they bounced homeward over the rough highway, Allan turned to Little John. "If we hadn't found out Prince John was just pretending he was poor, would you really have given him back all his gold?"

"Sure," replied Little John.

"But that would have made him rich again!" protested Allan.

Little John smiled. "Then it would have been okay for us to steal it all back!" he said. "It's a matter of principles!"

SOCCER: THE NEW KICK IN NORTH AMERICA

"It can't happen here!"

That's what everyone said. Everyone said that soccer would never become popular in North America. "Football is big. So is baseball, and hockey, and basketball. Soccer? Forget it!"

But everyone was wrong.

For many years, soccer has been hugely popular in more than 100 countries. In South America and Europe, crowds of over 100,000 people have jammed stadiums for important games. In Britain, fans of rival teams have started fights with each other. And when the World Cup matches are held—once every four years—businesses close down all over the globe as people head home to switch on their television sets. It is estimated that 1,000,000,000 (billion) people will follow the 1978 World Cup matches. Imagine—one *billion* soccer

fans! And until recently, only a very few of them lived in North America.

But very suddenly it seems, soccer *has* happened here. The year 1977 will probably be remembered as the year in which soccer "took off" in North America, especially as a spectator sport. However, even though it was not until 1977 that soccer achieved great popularity in North America, the sport has been played here for a long time. And a number of years of groundwork were necessary before soccer could become as popular as it has. A number of years of groundwork, and one very special player.

How did it all happen?

▶ THE GROUNDWORK

People have been playing soccer in North America since the time of the American

Revolution, 200 years ago. In cities with large immigrant populations, you could always see a soccer game in a park on a nice weekend day. Within the past few decades, many colleges and high schools have fielded soccer teams. Then in 1967 two professional soccer leagues were formed. But North American sports fans weren't ready for professional soccer. People didn't attend the games in large numbers. The leagues failed.

The leagues tried again in 1968. This time they joined together to become one league, the North American Soccer League (N.A.S.L.). But the N.A.S.L. didn't fare much better than the two original leagues had. At the end of the season, twelve of the seventeen teams in the league dropped out. Again, lack of fan support and money were the problems.

Yet despite these rather poor beginnings, the groundwork had been laid. In the late 1960's and early 1970's, more and more people began noticing soccer. In particular, the young people of North America were getting involved in the game. They were getting involved in the best way possible: they were playing it. And as more and more young people began playing soccer, the N.A.S.L. began to do a little better. Many of those youthful participants were also money-paying fans. So each year new teams came into the N.A.S.L.

▶ONE VERY SPECIAL PLAYER

By 1975 it was obvious that interest in professional soccer was growing. And more and more young people were playing on organized soccer teams. But soccer in North America still seemed to be missing something. It still needed something special before it would be considered a big-time sport.

Soccer found what it needed: a superstar, a player who could capture the attention of the fans, the newspapers, and the television cameras. His name? Edson Arantes do Nascimento, better known to the world as Pelé (pronounced pay-lay).

Although Pelé was discovered by North American soccer only in 1975, he had been known throughout the soccer-playing world since 1956. In that year, he began playing with the Santos team of Brazil (his native country) and very quickly became its star. No player alive could match his skills. Whether dribbling, shooting, passing, or "heading" the ball,

Pelé, the "Black Pearl," was the best. He was soccer's Babe Ruth: the great player beloved by all fans of the game. He was soccer's Muhammad Ali: a fabulous showman whom people came to watch even if they knew little about the sport. Pelé was just what North American professional soccer needed. In 1975 the owners of the New York Cosmos of the N.A.S.L. went after him with a $4,700,000 contract. Pelé had been ready to retire, but he signed on to play for three years.

It was not just money that brought Pelé here. He was already a wealthy man. But loving the game as much as he did, Pelé came because he wanted to help make soccer popular on this continent.

Pelé played his first game for the Cosmos in June, 1975. Since then, game by game, soccer's popularity has grown and grown. In 1977 record-setting crowds and nationwide television coverage have indeed proved that professional soccer has become a major sport in North America.

▶THE TURNSTILES ARE CLICKING

The Cosmos set a U.S. attendance record on June 19, 1977, when 62,394 fans passed through the turnstiles into Giants Stadium in East Rutherford, New Jersey. They saw Pelé score three goals as the Cosmos beat the Tampa Bay Rowdies, 3–1. Pelé says he cried that day—the sight of all those soccer fans had thrilled him to tears. "This," he said, "is what I came for."

However, that attendance record didn't stay on the books for long. On August 14, 1977, 77,691 people roared as the Cosmos trounced the Fort Lauderdale Strikers 8–3 in a playoff game. It was the largest crowd ever to attend a soccer match in North America.

Soccer is a team sport, and the Cosmos are a great team. They had other excellent players in addition to Pelé, including Italian star Giorgio Chinaglia and the masterful West German, Franz Beckenbauer. On August 28, in Portland, Oregon, the Cosmos faced the Seattle Sounders for the N.A.S.L. championship. The game, called the "Soccer Bowl," was televised in eleven countries including the United States. Seattle, a strong team, pressed the Cosmos from the opening kickoff. But the Cosmos held on to win, 2–1.

Steve Hunt, a 21-year-old Englishman, was

Pelé and Steve Hunt: The Cosmos are the champions!

the Cosmos' most valuable player that day. And goalie Shep Messing made some tough saves. For the Cosmos, winning the championship was the perfect way to finish the season. Overall, in 1977 the Cosmos drew an average attendance of 39,000 people per game.

The N.A.S.L. has eighteen teams, and five or six more are expected to join the league for the 1978 season. Despite the success of the Cosmos, not all the other teams are doing well. In 1977 the N.A.S.L. had an average attendance of 13,300 per game. Toronto, the 1976 champion, averaged only about 5,000 per game. And another league, the American Soccer League, with eight teams, averaged under 3,000 per game.

The people who run the professional soccer leagues are well aware of these attendance figures. They know, however, that as more and more young people take up the game, league attendance will naturally increase. So the professional soccer leagues have encouraged youth soccer leagues as much as possible.

▶ **PELÉ'S FAREWELL**

On October 1 the great Pelé played his final game. It was an exhibition match between the Cosmos and the Santos of Brazil, Pelé's first team. Pelé played the first half for the Cosmos and scored a goal. At halftime, he changed into a Santos shirt. He wanted to retire as a member of the Santos team.

After the game, which the Cosmos won, both teams declared that no player would ever again wear Pelé's number, 10, for either team. Pelé's great career was over.

With Pelé gone, will soccer continue to grow in North America? Undoubtedly it will. All the young people playing the game are sure that soccer has "made it."

More and more boys and girls are playing soccer—the game the whole world loves.

▶ THE BALL KEEPS MOVING

Indeed, youth soccer leagues are attracting hundreds of thousands of boys and girls each year. Youth soccer may soon have more participants than Little League baseball. And peewee football hasn't got a chance against the popularity of youth soccer.

What is it about soccer that draws so many young people to it? There are several things:

1. Anyone can play. Soccer is not only for the tall, strong, and heavy, as are football and basketball. Size doesn't matter. The smaller player can be just as good as the bigger player. And there are many leagues for girls as well as for boys.

2. There isn't much chance of injury in soccer, mostly because there is little body contact. In hockey and football, on the other hand, injuries are frequent.

3. Soccer doesn't require a lot of equipment; only a ball is necessary. Therefore, setting up a team is inexpensive. Parents of young hockey and football players have always complained about the costs of uniforms and protective padding and helmets. There is no such problem with soccer.

4. Playing soccer is excellent for getting into good physical condition. For 90 minutes, it's run, run, run. As one young player put it, "The ball keeps moving." And as the ball moves, the players must move after it. Compare this with the many delays and time-outs of football and basketball!

Most of all, soccer is a game that is filled with magic. It offers drama, excitement, and breathtaking speed. It's the game the whole world loves.

DANIEL J. DOMOFF
Consulting Editor
Educational Developmental Laboratories

SPACE BRIEFS

Two U.S. spacecraft, Voyagers 1 and 2, set out in 1977 to explore the outer reaches of the solar system. The unmanned vehicles will visit Jupiter and Saturn and their moons, and one spacecraft may even reach Uranus and Neptune. The Voyagers will travel for so long, to so many unexplored worlds, that children in 1977 will be adults before the mission is over.

Voyager 1 will approach Jupiter in March, 1979. Its twin sister ship, Voyager 2, will be about four months behind. If all goes well, the spacecraft will send television pictures back to earth as they pass the giant planet. The cameras will focus on a large red spot on Jupiter's gassy surface. The spot has puzzled scientists, who so far have been able to see it only through telescopes. The cameras will also scan the four largest of Jupiter's thirteen known moons, and may even discover a suspected fourteenth moon. Other instruments will study the chemical makeup of the planet and chart its magnetic fields.

Jupiter itself will give the Voyagers a boost on their way to the other planets. As Jupiter speeds along its orbit of the sun, its gravitational force will pull the Voyagers along, and then fling them out toward Saturn. If it were not for this "slingshot effect," the spacecraft would not be able to reach the ringed planet.

Experiments near Saturn will include a study of its rings, and of Titan, its largest moon. Titan is the only moon in the solar system known to have an atmosphere. In some ways the atmosphere is similar to Earth's.

If Voyager 1's mission near Saturn is successful, Voyager 2 will not have to pass so close to that planet. Then scientists will be able to aim the second ship so that it can take advantage of Saturn's "slingshot effect." Voyager 2 will then be headed out to explore Uranus and Neptune. It would reach Uranus in 1986, and Neptune in 1989, twelve years after having been launched.

Both Voyagers will eventually leave the solar system and wander forever through the universe. Each ship carries a message—just in case there are living beings out there to find it billions of years from now. The messages are on records telling what life is like on Earth. They also give examples of music (even rock-and-roll) and they carry greetings in many languages. One is from President Jimmy Carter. Part of it says, "This record represents our hope and our determination, and our goodwill in a vast and awesome universe."

The Voyager missions represent our attempt to better understand that universe.

An artist's conception of the Voyagers' journey to Jupiter and Saturn.

The first close look at
Phobos, a Martian moon.

An artist's conception of
a giant square solar sail.

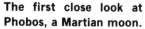
PHOBOS: A MARTIAN MOON

Phobos is not the most beautiful place ever seen. It is jagged, barren, dark, and covered with craters. Still, in 1977 scientists were very happy to get their first close look at it. Phobos is the larger of the two moons of Mars, and pictures of it were sent back to Earth by the Viking I spacecraft.

The pictures have given us the best look yet at another planet's moon. Scientists are excited about the pictures because they may be able to find out what Phobos is made of. And if scientists know that, they may also be able to learn how Phobos originated and where it came from.

Some scientists believe that Phobos is an asteroid—a small, planetlike body—that wandered too close to Mars and was captured by its gravity. Others think it was made from leftover material when Mars was first formed.

From the photographs, Phobos appears to be very much like an asteroid. As scientists examine them more closely, we will learn more about this Martian moon—and about the history of the solar system.

CLIPPER SHIPS

There are no breezes in space because there is no air. Why, then, is the National Aeronautics and Space Administration (NASA) building a sail-powered spacecraft? What will fill its sails and push it along? The answer may seem strange. It's sunlight.

Light rays are made up of little bundles of energy called photons. When light bounces off a surface, the photons give a small push—so small that people can't feel it. But when a lot of sunlight reflects off a huge, shiny sail, the many little pushes add up to a great force.

NASA is trying to build such a solar sail. It would be used to maneuver a spacecraft that contained cameras and scientific instruments. Solar clipper ships would be able to explore throughout the solar system, reaching speeds of 135,000 miles per hour (217,000 kilometers per hour), without needing any fuel.

Two kinds of solar sails are now under development. One kind is a giant square about a half mile (800 meters) long on each side, with a rigid frame to hold the sails. The spacecraft would sail along in outer space the way a wind-driven sailboat does in the water. The other kind of sail is a giant pinwheel called a heliogyro. It would have twelve sailcloth "blades," much like helicopter blades. Each would be 3½ miles (5,600 meters) long, and extremely narrow. Centrifugal force would keep the blades rigid. The entire spacecraft would spin through space. The sails for both designs would be made of a film of extremely thin plastic, coated with reflective aluminum.

In 1981, NASA plans to use a space shuttle to put the first clipper into orbit. The sail will be unfolded in space and the ship will be sent sailing for a rendezvous with Halley's comet, in 1986.

THE BATTLE OF SARATOGA

The crackling of musket fire echoed through the thick woodlands. Cannon boomed like thunderclaps, shaking the ground. Scarlet-coated British regulars charged, their bayonets glinting in the sun. On the opposite side of the field, buckskin-clad American riflemen riddled the British ranks with well-aimed volleys.

The fighting was desperate on that cool, clear September day in 1777. For more than three hours, the rival armies punched away at each other like enraged boxers.

When the fighting was over, the Americans retreated from the clearing around Freeman's Farm, near Saratoga, New York. General John Burgoyne's British army had won the day.

But they lost the war.

For the British had suffered heavy casualties at the battle of Freeman's Farm. And a few weeks later, the badly weakened British army was defeated in the final engagement of the Saratoga campaign. On October 17, 1777, General Burgoyne surrendered the battered remnants of his army to the American forces under General Horatio Gates. The series of military events that led to Burgoyne's surrender has come to be known as the Battle of Saratoga.

Few Americans know very much about Saratoga. Yet it was the turning point of the American Revolution, and it has been called "one of the most decisive victories in the history of mankind." Fewer still know that the real hero of Saratoga was a general named Benedict Arnold—the very same Benedict Arnold who later became a traitor.

In October, 1977, the 200th anniversary of the Battle of Saratoga was commemorated by several re-enactments of the fighting near the original site of the final battles. The story of the Saratoga campaign is an important one. It is worth remembering—and retelling.

It began in June, 1777, when General "Gentleman Johnny" Burgoyne and an army of over 9,000 men marched out of Canada and invaded New York. According to the British plan, Burgoyne's column was to move south to Albany, where it would be met by General William Howe's army coming north from New York City. A third British force, under Colonel Barry St. Leger, was to strike east from Oswego, on Lake Ontario. The combined British army would then sweep all the American troops from the Hudson-Champlain Valley.

British control of the strategic Hudson River would drive a wedge between New England and the other colonies. It was the old rule of divide and conquer.

At first the campaign went well for the British. Burgoyne's army sailed down Lake Champlain and attacked the American garrison at Fort Ticonderoga early in July. The outnumbered Americans were driven from the fort. By capturing Fort Ticonderoga, Burgoyne had opened a gateway to the Hudson.

But the Americans were far from beaten. The retreating rebel troops did everything they could to delay Burgoyne's advance. They chopped down trees and dug ditches to block the forest roads. So effective were the American tactics that in 23 days, Burgoyne was able to advance only 22 miles (35 kilometers).

As the British troops plunged deeper into the rugged wilderness, their troubles mounted. Supplies were running low. Farmers loyal to the Patriot cause burned their crops and drove off their cattle so the British wouldn't have food. By early August, Burgoyne's troops were exhausted and half-starved.

In desperation the British commander sent a detachment consisting mostly of Hessians (German mercenaries hired by the King of England to fight the Americans) on an expedition to gather food and fresh horses.

At Bennington, in what is now Vermont, the Hessians ran smack into a brigade of tough New England militiamen. The Americans whipped the Hessians, killing over 200 and capturing 700 more.

Almost at the same time, the British were suffering another defeat. Colonel St. Leger's column, marching east to join Burgoyne, was repulsed (at the Battle of Oriskany) by a hastily assembled force of local farmer-militiamen.

The two American victories were bitter blows to Burgoyne. To make matters worse, the British commander received word that General Howe was not marching north to support him as he had expected. Instead, Howe had decided to attack General George Washington's army in Pennsylvania.

This painting by John Trumbull shows Burgoyne presenting his sword (surrendering) to Gates.

Historians still debate why Howe did not go to Burgoyne's aid. Some claim that Howe never received the necessary orders from his superiors. In any event, Burgoyne now found himself isolated. He had no choice but to forge ahead and try to reach Albany on his own.

Between the British and Albany were some 9,000 American troops commanded by Major General Horatio Gates and his cheif lieutenant, General Benedict Arnold. The Americans were firmly dug in on a series of bluffs called Bemis Heights.

On September 19 Burgoyne sent three columns of British troops to assault the American positions. Gates was content to fight a defensive battle. But fiery Benedict Arnold finally persuaded the overcautious Gates to allow him to attack the British in the open, at Freeman's Farm.

Led by Arnold, the American troops fought the British to a standstill. Only the arrival of reinforcements late in the day saved the British from complete defeat.

Technically, the British won the battle, but they had lost hundreds of men, and the American rebels still blocked the way to Albany. The British hastily constructed some forts and waited, still hoping that General Howe would send troops to aid them.

When three weeks passed and no help came,

Burgoyne decided to gamble on another attack. On October 7, American and British troops clashed in the Second Battle of Freeman's Farm (also known as the Battle of Bemis Heights).

Again the battle was a seesaw affair. At a key moment, when the outcome was still in doubt, General Arnold galloped onto the field. Surveying the scene, Arnold discovered a weak point in the British line. He quickly gathered several American units and led them in a charge between two British redoubts (forts). Then the Americans swept into the Breymann Redoubt, the key to the British defenses, and captured it. In the fighting, Arnold was wounded in the leg. But by his bold action he had won the battle.

The British were now outflanked and had to retreat to Saratoga. There, outnumbered and surrounded, they surrendered ten days later.

The American victory at Saratoga had immediate impact. It lifted the morale of American Patriots. But most important, it led to an alliance between France and the rebelling colonies. With the aid of French troops and supplies, the American colonists went on to win their independence and to establish a new nation.

HENRY I. KURTZ
Author, *Captain John Smith*

ROSALYNN SMITH CARTER

Rosalynn Smith Carter was born in Plains, Georgia, on August 18, 1927. Her father, a Plains mechanic, died of leukemia when Rosalynn was 13. While her mother supported the family of four children by sewing for other people and working at the post office, Rosalynn helped by sewing and working in a beauty parlor. She attended high school in Plains and went to Georgia Southwestern College in nearby Americus, where she took a two-year general program in interior decorating.

Rosalynn and Jimmy Carter were married in 1946 immediately after Carter's graduation from the U.S. Naval Academy. During their first seven years of marriage, the Carters had three sons. (A daughter, Amy, was born in 1967.) Because her husband was often away for long tours of duty as a submarine officer, Rosalynn Carter reared the boys and managed the household.

When Carter left the Navy, he and Rosalynn returned to Plains to run the family farm and peanut business. Later, when Jimmy entered politics, Rosalynn continued to keep the books for the family business. She emerged as a public figure in her husband's second campaign for the governorship of Georgia. It was during this time that she became deeply interested in mental health, retardation, and the care of the aged. Her husband, as governor, placed her in charge of his administration's mental health program. Mrs. Carter became active in making legislative recommendations, recruiting volunteers, and informing the public of the necessity for mental health. She helped establish a statewide network of mental health centers.

Mrs. Carter is a rather shy and private person. Still, she became one of the most popular and sought-after speakers during her husband's two-year presidential campaign. A slender woman, with slightly curling brown hair, bright hazel eyes, and a warm engaging smile, Mrs. Carter captivated audiences wherever she traveled.

Perhaps her most significant role as first lady is that of adviser to her husband. Shortly after his election to the presidency in November, 1976, she took part in strategy sessions. She also joined in the discussions held to select presidential appointees, such as the cabinet officers. While she is not a policy-maker, the president does seek her ideas and advice on many issues.

Within the first few months of her husband's inauguration, Mrs. Carter set the tone for her role as first lady by appointing a "projects director" to help her carry out her ambitious and far-reaching plans. She does not limit her activities to hosting White House dinners, but takes a more active approach to her duties as the wife of a president. She does important work as a traveling ambassador for her husband, visiting those states and foreign countries that he is unable to visit. She also continues to play an important role as a political adviser in the Carter administration, and she works on mental health and problems of the elderly. Mrs. Carter serves as honorary chairperson of the President's Commission on Mental Health.

Reviewed by MARGARET B. KLAPTHOR
Smithsonian Institution

YOUTH IN ART

Have you ever looked at a painting and imagined that you were in it? This dream comes true for the lucky people who are selected each year as the live models who appear in the Pageant of the Masters. In this spectacular pageant, famous works of art are re-created using people and settings that are almost exactly like the original painting or sculpture. In 1977 the show included over 40 staged masterpieces, including paintings by El Greco, Edgar Degas, Salvador Dali, Winslow Homer, and John Singer Sargent.

This unusual show is held each year in a large outdoor amphitheater in Laguna Beach, California. It is staged every evening for 45 days during the summer. The first pageant of "living pictures" was held in 1933, and since then it has become well known all over the world.

▶ RE-CREATING THE ARTWORKS

A special committee selects the artworks that are to be re-created for the pageant. Once the selection is made, photographs are taken of the paintings and sculpture. These photographs are used to guide the artists who will paint or construct huge copies of the artworks. Each copy is proportionately scaled so that it will appear human-sized on the stage.

▶ THE LIVE MODELS

About 150 live models star in the cast every night. (There are two complete casts because each person is in the show seven nights straight, and then gets a week off.) Many factors are considered in selecting the models, who are all volunteers. People of all ages are used. But a person's size and shape are more important than age, because the model must be in perfect proportion to the painted background.

To be chosen to appear in one of the masterpieces is quite an honor, and young people are often selected. In the 1977 pageant the youngest stars were 9 years old.

▶ COSTUMING

Costuming and makeup are very important. They can easily turn a boy or a girl into an old man or woman. The costumes are made from unbleached muslin cloth, which is painted to match the colors and shadows of the original artwork. The costumes are stiffened so that they will remain motionless during the performance, even if a breeze is blowing.

▶ ON STAGE

The exciting pageant is ready to begin. The announcer tells the audience about the artwork that is soon to be seen. As he speaks, stagehands are quietly arranging the settings behind the curtain. The models are helped into position, sometimes hanging onto hidden supports so they won't lose their position when the curtain is open.

Then the orchestra begins and the curtain opens. The special stage lighting focuses on the large-scale "artwork" and helps make the stage picture look like the original. The audience gasps and applauds, amazed that the "painting" or "sculpture" before them is a giant re-creation.

This is the most difficult time for the models, because they must remain perfectly still. A sneeze or cough would ruin the show. Finally, after a minute or so, the curtain closes and the models relax. They go back to the dressing room, and the next work of art prepares for its showing.

The two-hour pageant traditionally ends with a famous work that requires thirteen models. It's *The Last Supper,* a magnificent painting by Leonardo da Vinci.

▶ THE CAST SAYS . . .

The first evening of the Pageant of the Masters has ended. It's been a happy and dazzling experience for both the audience and the cast.

Let's see what one of the cast members has to say about the pageant. Dave Strauss, age 14, was chosen as a live model in 1977, when he appeared in gleaming gold body makeup. Dave was one of three models who portrayed the carved figures on a gold comb from ancient Scythia, now displayed in a Soviet museum. "The makeup is pretty messy," says Dave, "but I think being in the pageant is neat, and so do my friends."

Turn the page and you will see how the oil painting *Happy Days*, by Eugene Iverd, was re-created.

MICHELE AND TOM GRIMM
Authors, *Hitchhiker's Handbook*

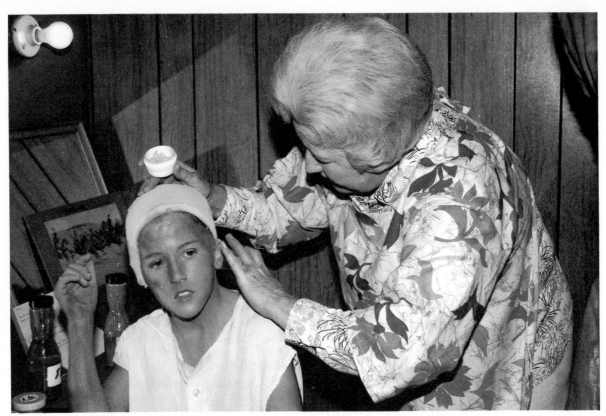

Makeup: the live models will appear very much like the people in the painting *Happy Days*.

Setting up: the models are placed against the backdrop of the re-created artwork.

The stage picture: the re-created artwork *Happy Days* as the audience sees it.

The real picture: the actual painting *Happy Days* by Eugene Iverd.

ANIMALS IN THE NEWS

It seems as if everybody is playing Frisbee—even dogs! This is Ashley Whippet, who set a world record by dashing 106 yards (97 meters) to catch a flying Frisbee with his teeth.

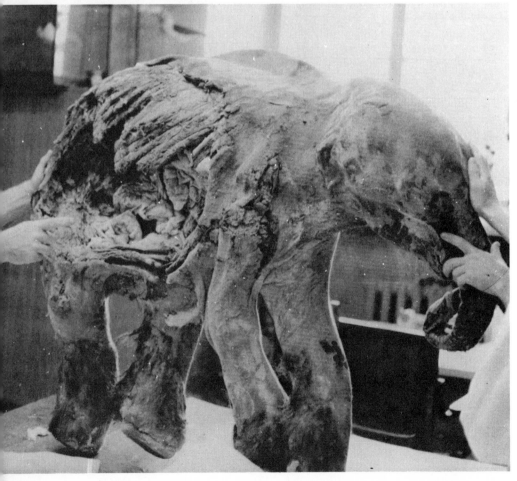

Mammoths are prehistoric relatives of the elephant. In 1977 the frozen remains of a baby mammoth were found at an excavation site in northeastern Siberia. Scientists believe that it died about 10,000 years ago. After it has been examined and studied, the mammoth will be stuffed and put on display in a museum in the Soviet Union.

To win the Triple Crown of horse racing, a horse must win the Kentucky Derby, the Preakness, and the Belmont Stakes—all in the same year. Only ten horses have ever done it. This is Seattle Slew, who did it in 1977. Seattle Slew also set a record—he won the Triple Crown without having lost any race prior to winning the "Big Three."

In 1977, Dersade Bobby's Girl became the new reigning queen of dogdom: the Sealyham terrier was chosen best in show at the Westminster Kennel Club show—the most important dog event in the United States.

ENERGY-CONSERVATION PATENTS

Energy crunch! Energy crisis! Energy conservation! These are the cries we hear every day from scientists, public officials, and statesmen as they try to design a program to solve the world's growing energy shortage.

We need petroleum for making gasoline to drive our cars, diesel fuel to run our trains and trucks, oil to heat our homes, and many useful chemicals. But the supply of petroleum is becoming scarce and the same is true of natural gas. At the same time, the need for energy is continually increasing as the world's population grows and as more countries become industrialized.

Other sources of energy, such as solar, nuclear, wind, and geothermal energy, are now being developed and expanded. But until they are fully developed, we are all urged to use less energy and to use it more efficiently. We should drive our cars less, ride in car pools, use public transportation, insulate our homes, and keep the thermostat down in home, office, and factory.

These are just some of the ways that people are trying to conserve energy today. But long before today's energy crisis struck, ingenious inventors were coming up with imaginative ideas to accomplish the same purpose. Some of them thought of ways to travel without using a single drop of gasoline or a single watt of electricity. We find their ideas embodied in inventions for which they obtained patents as long as 100 years ago.

A patent is a document granted to an inventor by the government. Even a child can get one. The patent gives the inventor the exclusive rights to his or her invention for a fixed number of years. This means that no one else can make, use, or sell the invention without the inventor's permission.

Many patents have been granted for inventions intended to conserve energy. Here are some early ones that are quite ingenious and amusing.

HARRY GOLDSMITH
Former Patent Counsel

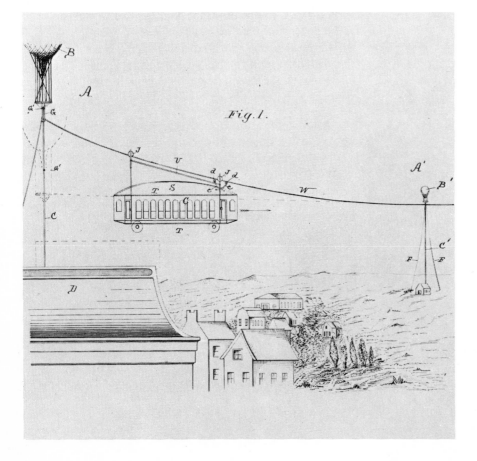

Fig. 1.

The Aerial Railway and Car was patented in 1885. Balloons, soaring high above the earth, are anchored to the ground along the route you want to travel. A cable connects the balloons. Suspended from the cable is a cable car carrying passengers. To make the car move along the cable, the ballons are raised or lowered to incline the cable properly. By the energy of its own weight—that is, by gravity—the car will travel down the cable from one station to the next, somewhat like a child zooming down a slide.

An Aerial Auto was patented in 1887, in which living motors replace mechanical ones. In this invention eagles, vultures, or condors are connected to the vehicle by a special harness. When the giant birds flap their wings, they are able to drive the auto in any direction.

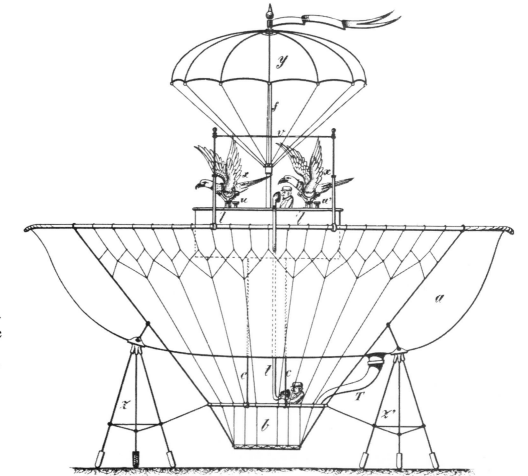

Visitors to Disneyland cruise past the unique topiary garden that welcomes them to Fantasyland's *It's a Small World*.

GREEN ANIMALS

A giraffe that can't bend its neck. A bear that won't chase you. An elephant that can't move its trunk. A swan that can't swim. A hippopotamus that can't walk.

Is this an animal hospital? No, it's a garden where all these animals are green. Though they look like animals, they are really green plants that have been given animal forms.

The art of shaping plants into special forms is called topiary gardening. Some topiary shapes are fairly simple to create, such as a tree in the shape of a ball or a pyramid. Other shapes are more difficult to achieve. It may take five or six years to create a large animal, such as a bear or an elephant.

Not every plant can be trained into a topiary form. The best plants to use are trees and bushes with small, closely packed leaves or needles, such as boxwood and privet yew.

To keep topiary sculpture in shape, they must be pruned—the branches, twigs, and leaves that aren't needed must be cut off. Pruning has to be done several times a year, or that giraffe will grow a beard, and the elephant's trunk will get very, very long.

▶ **A UNIQUE TOPIARY GARDEN**

Topiary gardening is a very ancient art, begun by the Romans. It reached its greatest popularity in England, some 300 years ago. Today many fine topiary forms can still be seen in English gardens.

One of the most famous topiary gardens in the United States is at Disneyland in California. Here you can see a Disneyworld of green animals in a lovely gardenlike setting.

The Disney method of topiary is unique. When the garden was first being planned, it was realized that the usual topiary varieties of trees and bushes would take too long to grow to figure-styling size. So experts experimented and came up with certain varieties of junipers and conifers. These varieties

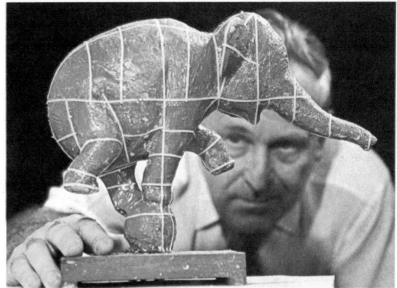

A scale model is the first step in designing a topiary animal. Then shrubs are trained to grow around a lightweight steel "skeleton." It usually takes several years to achieve the desired shape.

An elephant.

A giraffe.

grow fast and can be trimmed frequently without being harmed. Walt Disney called this method "instant topiary."

If you visit Disneyland you can see juniper elephants, alligators of golden thuja, boxwood hippos, and bears of Japanese yew. The green animals are given more care and attention than most animals in a zoo. They are carefully bathed, fed, doctored, and barbered. Says one Disney landscape gardener, "The topiary figures are our special pets. I guess you might say it's because they have a tendency to grow on you."

▶ YOU CAN MAKE YOUR OWN GREEN ANIMAL

You don't neeed a large garden or big bushes to practice topiary gardening. Plant a small boxwood in a pot and keep it indoors or on a patio. By carefully pruning it and using wires to train it, you can slowly create an unusual shape. It may take a fair amount of time and patience, but you might be the first person in your neighborhood to have a green animal as a pet.

Pampered pets at a dog show: being squirted with hair spray . . .

. . . keeping clean in a playpen . . .

PAMPERED PETS

Have you ever seen a dog getting its eyelashes trimmed or its toenails cut? Or a dog with its head protected by a bonnet? Just go to a dog show. There, everything is done to take special care of dogs when they are competing for ribbons and top honors.

Dog shows are held all over the world. In some places, there are shows every weekend. Not all the shows are as fancy or as famous as the Westminster Kennel Club show, which has been held every year in New York City for the past 100 years. But wherever the show is held, you'll see plenty of pampered pets.

Because they are judged on the beauty of their coats, the dogs are carefully washed and groomed before they arrive for the show. To keep them clean, the dogs' owners sometimes carry them or wheel them around in cages so their paws won't get dirty. Other dogs wear little bootees on their feet. Even playpens are used to keep the dogs off the ground while they wait their turn to be exhibited.

You'll see dogs wearing bibs so that food won't spill on their shiny coats. After being combed and brushed, some dogs get a squirt of hair spray to keep everything in place. And scissors are always kept handy for a last-minute trim.

After long hours of training and grooming, the dogs are ready for the show, which is a big elimination contest. First the judges look for the dog that best represents the standard for its breed. Then there are still more eliminations, until that one outstanding animal is selected Best in Show—the greatest honor. For that lucky dog and its owner, all the training and pampering have paid off.

MICHELE AND TOM GRIMM
Authors, *What Is a Seal?*

. . . its head protected with a bonnet.

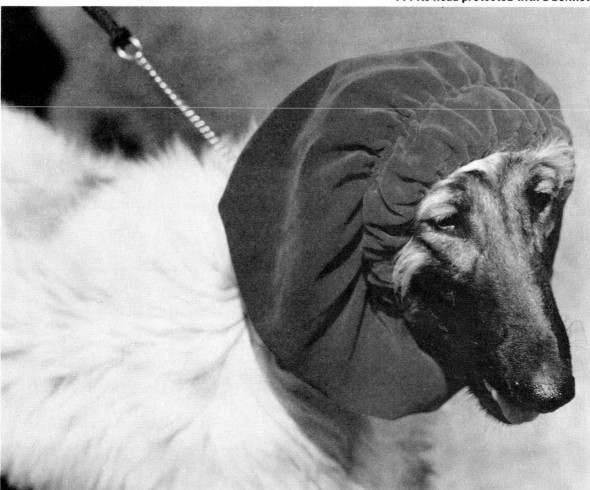

YOUNG PHOTOGRAPHERS

A good photograph is like a dream captured. That's what today's young photographers seem to be showing us, whether the subject is a cityscape, a rural landscape, or a purely made-up pattern. Mood and atmosphere are all-important, and if the young photographers convey these to you in their pictures, then their work is a success. The photographs on these pages are all prize winners in the Scholastic Photography Awards program of 1977. The program is sponsored by the Eastman Kodak Company.

Earthquake, by Scott Headley, 15, Rochester, New York

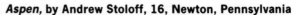

Aspen, by Andrew Stoloff, 16, Newton, Pennsylvania

Rock & Roll, **by Curt Breusing, 17,**
Anaheim, California

Skyline, **by John Craig, 17, Cincinnati, Ohio**

Layered Forest, by Richard Oren, 17, Tucson, Arizona

Contemplation,
by Alice Larson, 18,
Plainview, Texas

Hair in the Air, by Charlie Clement, 18,
Hebron, Connecticut

Abandoned Reaper,
by Kevin Farrell, 17,
Oak Lawn, Illinois

IS ANYBODY OUT THERE?

A great whirlwind surrounded by fire came out of the north. From its midst came four creatures. They looked somewhat like people, but each had four faces, those of a man, a lion, an ox, and an eagle. Each creature had four wings and brass-colored feet that resembled a calf's.

These awe-inspiring creatures were described by the Prophet Ezekiel thousands of years ago. But throughout the ages, writers and artists have described their visions of fan-

tastical creatures. When presented as being scientifically possible, these descriptions are called science fiction. And yet, is it really fiction? Maybe there are such creatures—living, intelligent beings in outer space, with whom people on Earth can communicate.

Many scientists think this is possible. They believe that ours isn't the only advanced civilization in the universe. The scientists point out that there are probably millions and millions of other planets in the universe, revolving around suns, or stars, much like our own sun. Many of these planets probably have environmental conditions that would support some sort of life, resembling bacteria perhaps. But on some planets, there might be intelligent creatures much more advanced than Earth's human beings.

How can we find these intelligent beings? Scientists are using three methods in their search: sending unmanned spacecraft, sending messages, and listening for messages.

In 1972 the United States launched a spacecraft called Pioneer 10. It traveled toward Jupiter, which it passed in 1973, sending back a lot of valuable information about the giant planet. Pioneer 10 continued on its path away from Earth. A few years from now it will leave our solar system, on an endless journey toward other stars and planets. Maybe a strange civilization will see and capture it. In case that happens, scientists have put a message on board the spacecraft. The message, engraved on an aluminum plaque, includes pictures of a woman and a man and diagrams of facts about Earth, the rest of our solar system, and the hydrogen atom. This was the first attempt to send a written message into outer space.

Another kind of message was placed aboard a Voyager spacecraft that was launched in 1977. The Voyager is expected to pass by Jupiter, Saturn, and Uranus. After twelve years in our solar system, it too will pass into outer space. The Voyager carries a record player and a copper record. The recorded message includes greetings in 60 different languages, and even from some whales. Also on the record are coded signals that can be turned into 116 photos of people, things, and places on Earth. Then there is a sequence of Earth sounds, such as earthquakes, rain, wind, a baby's cry, cars, planes. Most of the record is music—a variety that includes Bach, Beethoven, Chuck Berry, and a Peruvian wedding song.

Don't expect to hear next year—or even in your lifetime—that another civilization has received these messages. Our solar system's *nearest* neighbor is the star Alpha Centauri. It will take the Voyager 40,000 years to reach this star, and perhaps millions of years before it nears a place inhabited by intelligent beings.

Since messages in spacecraft take so very long to reach another part of the universe, some scientists believe this isn't the best way to contact other beings. They believe we should listen for, and send, signals, which travel much faster than spacecraft.

About 1960, scientists decided that the best signals to use were radio signals. Radio signals, or radio waves, travel at the speed of light—186,282 miles (300,000 kilometers) per second. In addition to traveling very fast, radio waves are not usually lost or weakened as they move through the atmosphere or outer space.

The United States space agency (NASA) has recommended a project called SETI—*S*earch for *E*xtra*t*errestrial *I*ntelligence. The project would be carried out over a period of six years by two research teams.

The researchers would use radiotelescopes to "listen" for radio waves coming from space. One team would map the part of the sky that is visible over the southwestern United States. The second team would listen to stars that lie within 100 light years of Earth. (A light year is the distance that light travels in a year—which is about 6 trillion miles, or 9.5 trillion kilometers.)

As you may know, radio waves have many different frequencies. Think what problems you would have if a friend told you to listen to a special radio program tonight, but didn't tell you what station, or frequency, to tune to. Like your radio, a telescope can be tuned to only one frequency at a time. The SETI scientists would listen to either of two radio frequencies. One is the frequency of the radio waves given off by hydrogen atoms. The other is the frequency of the combination of one hydrogen atom and one oxygen atom, called the hydroxyl radical. Scientists reason that if there are scientists on other planets, they might guess that these radio frequencies are the best "channels" of interplanetary communication.

Other projects have already listened for radio waves from outer space. So far, all they have heard have been hissing and crackling

sounds. These are the constant noises that radio telescopes pick up from anywhere in space.

Sending messages with radio signals is faster than sending them in spacecraft, but it still takes a long, long time—if it works at all. Even a message from a planet in a fairly nearby solar system would take 200 years to reach us. As one scientist commented, "They say 'Hello, how are you?' and 200 years later they hear us say, 'Fine!' It's not what you would call a snappy dialogue!"

Of course there's always the chance that creatures from outer space may come to visit us. Some people think this has already happened. But most scientists put more faith in spacecraft and radiotelescopes than in reports of encounters with flying saucers and whirlwinds surrounded by fire.

LINCOLN LORE

If you were asked to choose the greatest U.S. president, who would it be? Recently the U.S. Historical Society asked a group of leading American historians to list the top ten presidents of the United States. The 85 scholars who responded all picked Abraham Lincoln to head the list as the greatest U.S. president.

The others who ranked in the top ten were George Washington, Franklin D. Roosevelt, Theodore Roosevelt, Thomas Jefferson, Woodrow Wilson, Andrew Jackson, Harry S. Truman, James K. Polk, and John Adams.

But Abraham Lincoln stands head and shoulder above them all. More than 100 years after an assassin's bullet struck him down, he remains a towering figure in American history. To millions of Americans, the 16th president is still number one.

A beardless Lincoln. Our image of Abraham Lincoln is that of a man with a beard. Actually, he didn't grow his familiar whiskers until after he was nominated as the Republican candidate for president in 1860. Until he was 51, he had been clean-shaven.

Lincoln might have remained beardless if it had not been for an 11-year-old girl. Her name was Grace Bedell and she lived in the town of Westfield, New York. On October 15, 1860, the youngster wrote a letter to Lincoln suggesting that he grow a beard. "You would look a great deal better for your face is so thin," Grace advised. "All the ladies like whiskers and they would tease their husbands to vote for you and then you would be President."

Lincoln replied on October 19. He thanked Grace for her "very agreeable letter." As for her suggestion, he pointed out that he had never worn whiskers and if he grew them now, people might think it a "silly affectation."

However, Lincoln gave the matter more thought. And he grew the beard that he would wear throughout his presidency.

In February, 1861, while on his way to Washington, Lincoln stopped off at Westfield. Grace Bedell was among those who greeted him. Lincoln kissed her on the cheek, pointed to his new whiskers, and told her: "I grew them just for you."

The print shown here is one of the two remaining copies of a Lincoln portrait given out to delegates at the Republican National Convention in 1860.

BATILLUS

Batillus, a new seagoing oil tanker built for Société Maritime Shell, is the largest moving object ever built. The tanker, which can carry 550,000 tons of cargo, measures about 1,358 feet (414 meters) in length and 241 feet (73 meters) in height. These measurements make it slightly taller than, and twice as long as, the Houston Astrodome. *Batillus* is fitted with just about every piece of sophisticated technical equipment ever designed by marine engineers. If the ship runs into trouble and breaks down at sea, it may have to be towed to one of only six dry docks in the world that can repair a ship of this size.

TUT, THE BOY KING

The ancient Egyptians believed that "you *can* take it with you." In fact, they believed that you *had* to—if you wanted to be ready for your next life.

And so royalty and other wealthy people built large burial tombs. These contained not just the body of the dead person but all sorts of things the person might need or want in the next life: furniture, weapons, jewelry, religious objects, food, sandals, musical instruments, and incense. The more important the person, the bigger the tomb and the richer its contents.

We cannot say if this practice helped the dead. But it was a wonderful practice as far as people living today are concerned. Objects buried in tombs, if they were not stolen by grave robbers, were preserved and kept safe for thousands of years. When the tombs were discovered in the 19th and 20th centuries, they revealed important information about what life was like in ancient Egypt.

The richest discovery of all was the most recent. This was the discovery in 1922 of the tomb of Tutankhamen, a king who ruled Egypt more than 3,300 years ago—probably from about 1334 B.C. to about 1325 B.C. Some 5,000 objects were found in his tomb. Fifty-five of the most splendid of these objects are now touring the United States in an exhibit called "Treasures of Tutankhamen."

Tutankhamen—or Tut, as he is now often called—was only 9 years old when he ascended the throne. While still a child, he married Ankhesenamen, a daughter of Nefertiti. And then suddenly, when he was only 18 or 19, King Tut died. The cause of his death is not known. However, his skull is somewhat damaged, which suggests that he might have been assassinated.

It was the practice in ancient Egypt to mummify the body. This involved several steps. First, all the internal organs except the heart were removed. A mineral called natron was used to dry the body. Then oils and other substances were used to embalm it. Finally, the body was wrapped in linen and placed in a coffin. King Tut's body was actually placed in three coffins, one inside the other. The innermost coffin—that closest to the body—was made of solid gold.

King Tut's internal organs were embalmed separately. The liver, lungs, stomach, and intestines were placed in four miniature coffins, each guarded by a golden statue of a goddess.

The ancient Egyptians buried their royalty in an area along the Nile River called the Valley of the Kings. There, probably after a lavish funeral, King Tut's mummy and belongings were placed in a tomb, which was then sealed. Not too long afterward, robbers broke into the tomb. They stole some gold and jewels and the precious oils and unguents (ointments) that filled vases and jars. But most of the tomb's contents was left behind. As time passed, the sands of the hot, windy valley covered the tomb, hiding it from later bands of robbers.

In the 19th century, archeologists began digging in the valley, looking for tombs. They found more than 30 royal tombs. All of them had been robbed, so they contained relatively few treasures. By the beginning of the 20th century, most archeologists believed that all the tombs in the valley had been discovered. But one young archeologist disagreed.

Howard Carter believed that the tomb of King Tut was somewhere in the Valley of the Kings. He based this belief, in part, on several earlier finds: a cup bearing King Tut's name; a group of pottery jars bearing Tut's seal; and a small tomb containing pictures of Tut and his wife.

Carter convinced a fellow Britisher, Lord Carnarvon, to finance a search for the tomb. In 1918, work began. By 1922, Carnarvon became discouraged. He said he would not finance another year of sifting through sand. Carter pleaded for one last season, and Carnarvon agreed.

On November 4, 1922, the Egyptians who worked for Carter discovered the beginning of a staircase. As they cleared away the overlying material, they came upon a door sealed with the seals of the royal burial place. Carter telegraphed Carnarvon, telling him of the discovery and urging him to come to Egypt.

Carnarvon arrived in Egypt on November 20. By November 26, the door was removed, revealing a passageway that ended in another sealed door. Carter drilled a small hole in the second door and looked in.

"Can you see anything?" asked Lord Carnarvon. "Yes, wonderful things," replied Carter.

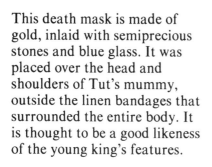

This death mask is made of gold, inlaid with semiprecious stones and blue glass. It was placed over the head and shoulders of Tut's mummy, outside the linen bandages that surrounded the entire body. It is thought to be a good likeness of the young king's features.

Carter was looking into the antechamber, the first of four small rooms in the tomb. It was piled high with all sorts of objects—thrones, beds, boxes, weapons, even chariots.

Slowly the men made their way through the antechamber, the annex, the burial chamber, and the treasury. Each room contained priceless treasures.

"The period to which the tomb belongs is in many respects the most interesting in the whole history of Egyptian art," Carter wrote, "and we were prepared for beautiful things. What we were not prepared for was the astonishing vitality and animation which characterized certain of the objects."

The most beautiful of all the objects was found in Tut's coffin. There, covering the King's mummy, was a death mask made of solid gold and inlaid with stones and glass. Its features are those of the young king who lived so very long ago: narrow eyes edged with black, a slender nose, fleshy lips.

The mummy itself was in poor condition. The oils used to preserve the body had partly destroyed it. But we must be thankful for the riches with which the body was surrounded. If the Egyptians hadn't believed that utensils, ornaments, and furnishings were needed in the afterlife, we could never have learned so much about young King Tut and his time.

117

This elegant statue of the goddess Selket is made of wood covered with gold. On her head is her emblem, a scorpion. The Egyptians believed that Selket had magical powers. The statue was placed in Tut's tomb to protect his mummy against evil.

This small chair is made of ebony and decorated with ivory and gold. Its legs are shaped like the paws of a lion. The chair was probably made for Tut when he was a young boy.

The ancient Egyptians liked ornate jewelry. This beautiful pendant is made of gold, semiprecious stones, and glass. The yellowish scarab in the center is a symbol of the sun god. The scarab has the wings, tail, and hind legs of a falcon, another symbol of the sun god.

A lion sits atop this cosmetic jar that contained scented oils and unguents. Perhaps the lion was meant to suggest the character of King Tut. Or it may represent the god Bes, who was a god of pleasure. The contents of such jars were considered very precious and were removed by ancient robbers who broke into Tut's tomb.

THE MYSTERY OF THE MISSING MONA

"So that's the famous Mona Pizza," Mickey said, looking up at the framed painting over Sir Hillary Dillary Dock's fireplace.

"The most valuable painting in London," replied the wealthy art collector. "It's worth *millions*! If anybody stole it . . ."

"You have nothing to worry about," Mickey assured Sir Hillary. "Sleuth is checking all the doors and windows right now! He'll make sure your burglar alarm is working perfectly!"

Sir Hillary breathed a sigh of relief. "I'm certainly glad I thought of calling in Sleuth after I bought the Mona Pizza," he said. "If *anybody* can protect my painting, it's England's Greatest Detective!"

Down the hall, Sleuth was carefully inspecting the burglar alarm wires with his magnifying glass. Inch by inch, he scanned the red and green strands, making sure they were in perfect order. He followed the wires down the hallway, not noticing he was approaching a mirror. Suddenly he was in front of the mirror, still holding the magnifying glass to his eye.

Through the magnifying glass, Sleuth stared at his own eye, five times bigger than normal. Thanks to his early training to react quickly in times of danger, the Great Detective leaped backward with a shriek, crashed through the burglar-alarm-wired window behind him, and landed with a thud in the bed of geraniums under the window. The burglar alarm worked perfectly.

CLANGALANGALANGALANG!

In the library, Mickey and Sir Hillary jumped to their feet. "It's a burglar!" Sir Hillary exclaimed, dashing out of the library and down the hall, with Mickey hot on his heels.

Reaching the broken window, they looked outside. Their puzzled gaze fell upon England's Greatest Detective, spread-eagled among the pink and red geraniums. "Gentlemen," he announced, "the Mona Pizza is safe! There is nothing wrong with the burglar alarm!"

Meanwhile, a strange scene was taking place across town, at the infamous College of Criminal Knowledge. Armadillo, Sidney, and Fliplip were standing in front of Professor Nefarious. What's so strange about that? Well, at this particular moment, Armadillo, Sidney, and Fliplip were dressed in track suits, and each was holding a very long pole!

"Your assignment for today," the Professor was saying, "is to learn how to pole-vault!"

"I thought we was gonna steal the Mona Pizza," said Sidney.

"Yeah, boss," whined Armadillo, very disappointed in the respectability of the assignment.

"We *are* going to steal the Mona Pizza," the Professor snapped. "That's what the poles are for! You're going to pole-vault up on Sir Hillary's roof tonight!"

"Huh?" said the three track-suited crooks.

The Professor smiled evilly. "The roof and the chimney are the only places in Sir Hillary's mansion that are not connected to the burglar alarm!"

Late that night, the Professor drove his students to the wall surrounding Sir Hillary's mansion. He waited as his three henchmen scrambled over the wall and dashed toward the mansion with their long poles.

The first one to vault up on the roof was Sidney. He carried a bucket of water, which, as soon as he reached the roof, he poured down the chimney, just in case there was a fire going in the fireplace below. Next up, a long rope and a laundry bag over his arm, was Fliplip. Last up was Armadillo. Sidney and Armadillo tied the rope around Fliplip's waist and proceeded to lower him down the chimney.

Outside the mansion's iron gate, the Professor watched the operation. "It's all going perfectly," he snickered.

Inside the house, Fliplip picked himself up from the sooty fireplace and began his search for the priceless Mona Pizza. Suddenly, above the fireplace, right behind him, he saw it!

Fliplip climbed on the mantle, removed the painting from its frame, and stuffed it into the

laundry bag. Then he tugged on the rope around his waist.

On the roof, Sidney and Armadillo felt the tug. "There's the signal! He's got it!" Sidney whispered excitedly, giving the rope a vigorous yank!

Fliplip and his laundry bag flew out of the chimney like a cannonball out of a cannon!

"I got it! I got it!" he exclaimed, zooming straight up over the heads of his two astonished partners! When he came down, he missed the roof and landed with an enormous splash in the muddy bottom of Sir Hillary's fish pond!

Since Sidney and Armadillo were holding the other end of the rope around Fliplip's waist, they, too, tumbled off the roof and joined Fliplip in the pond! Wet and muddy, the three crooks struggled out of the pond and raced toward the mansion wall.

"We got it, Perfesser!" they reported, as they clambered over the wall and into the Professor's waiting car.

"It's gone!" wailed Sir Hillary the next morning, staring up at the empty frame over his fireplace. He turned to Sleuth. "You told me the Mona Pizza was safe! And now it's gone! What kind of a detective are you, *anyway*?"

"I am England's Greatest Detective!" the Great Man replied huffily.

"Then *find my painting*!" Sir Hillary demanded.

"Look here, Sleuth," Mickey interrupted, kneeling in front of the fireplace. "Sooty footprints! The crook must have come down the chimney!"

"Aha!" exclaimed Sleuth. "Footy sootprints! That means the crook must have come down the chimney!"

"That's how he avoided the burglar alarm," Sir Hillary added.

"There may be more clues outside," Mickey said, heading for the front door.

Over by the wall, Mickey was the first to discover the three long poles.

"Aha!" Sleuth said, applying his magnifying glass to Mickey's discovery. "Stilts! That's how the crook got on the roof!"

"But there are *three* of them, Sleuth," Mickey said. "I don't know of any three-legged crooks in London, do you?"

Sleuth thought for a moment. "No," he answered.

Sleuth returned to examining the three mysterious poles. "Aha" he suddenly exclaimed, peering through his magnifying glass at the end of one of the poles. "There's something written on these poles! It says, 'PROPERTY OF THE COLLEGE OF CRIMINAL KNOWLEDGE SPORTS DEPARTMENT (POLE-VAULTING DIVISION)!' "

Mickey grabbed the detective by the coattail.

"Come on, Sleuth! I think you've solved the case of the missing Mona!"

"Naturally," Sleuth said, wondering what Mickey was talking about.

Back at the College of Criminal Knowledge, joy was unrestrained. "We did it, boys!" the Professor said with triumph in his voice. "We got the *Mona Pizza!*"

"Where are you going to hang it, Perfesser?" Fliplip asked.

"*Hang* it! We're going to *sell* it, you numbskull!" the Professor boomed.

A knock on the door prevented Fliplip from getting a knock on the head.

The Professor tossed the priceless canvas to Fliplip. "Quick! Hide the painting!" he ordered as he opened the front door.

"Laundry man," said the white-suited man on the porch. "Somebody named Nefarious called and said you have some muddy, sooty track suits to be picked up."

The Professor grabbed the laundry bag from his desk top and shoved it into the laundry man's hands. "Thank you and good-bye!" he said to the intruder, pushing him out of the doorway and closing the door after him.

He turned to Fliplip. "Now then . . . where's the painting?" Fliplip swallowed hard. "I hid it with the dirty clothes!"

Around the gills, Professor Nefarious turned a bright green. "You idiot!" he screamed at the rapidly retreating Flip. "After all the trouble we went to to steal the Mona Pizza, *YOU GAVE IT TO THE LAUNDRY MAN?!*"

"No," Fliplip answered. *"You* did."

"That confession was all we needed!" said a familiar voice behind him. The Professor whirled around and came face to face with Sleuth, Mickey, and six London policemen standing in the open doorway.

"Hand over the painting," Mickey commanded. "We know you have it."

"No, we don't," smiled the Professor. "And you can't prove a thing without the Mona Pizza!"

Suddenly, the laundry man appeared in the door. In his hand, he held the Mona Pizza! "By the way, Professor," he said, "I forgot to ask you. Do you want starch in this painting?"

INDEX

ILLUSTRATION CREDITS AND ACKNOWLEDGMENTS